LinguaForum TOEFL® *i*BT

Core Topic Guide

Vol. 2

Social
Sciences

LinguaForum™

LinguaForum TOEFL® *i*BT

Core Topic Guide

VOLUME 2

Social **Sciences**

For information about the *Core Topic Guide* series, email us at
info@linguastudy.com

ISBN: 89-5563-086-7   54740

R/N (CRctTFRHS02): 07180530EB/08080530EB/12080530EB/03020630EB/04100630EB

About Core Topic Guide

Core Topic Guide is a four book series designed to provide intermediate to advanced English language learners with essential background knowledge for all major subjects appearing on the Next Generation TOEFL® (*i*BT) test.

The *Core Topic Guide* series has four books:
History & the Arts: **Volume 1**
Social Sciences: **Volume 2**
Biology, Archeology, & Anthropology: **Volume 3**
Empirical Sciences: **Volume 4**

About the Books

- Each book in the *Core Topic Guide* series contains sixty high interest and high relevance reading passages designed to increase a student's background knowledge of TOEFL® topics.
- Each passage is fully supported with footnotes to explain idiomatic language and references to events or people which may be culturally unfamiliar.
- Each passage has several reading comprehension questions, complete with answer key, to ensure comprehension by the students.

By providing students with essential background knowledge of TOEFL® topics, as well as giving them valuable experience reading academic writing, *Core Topic Guide* increases a TOEFL® test taker's comfort level at test time.

LinguaForum Research Center

Contents

IV Sociology

V Communications

SOCIAL SCIENCES

Basic **Economics**

I

1.1 The 17th-18th Century: Wampum

● *Coin* can also be used as a verb to describe the process of making money.

What did Native Americans in North America use for money? They did not use paper money or gold or silver coins, as Europeans did. Instead, they "coined●" their money from a seemingly strange source: clam shells.

A clam called the "quohog" had a shell that was purple and white on the inside. Native Americans made beads from the **lining** of the quohog shell and from another shell called a "periwinkle." These beads were called "wampum" and served as money. Colors ranged from white to deep purple or black. A deep purple bead was worth most of all. It was worth twice as much as a white bead of wampum. The beads differed in size but were approximately as big as rice grains. The wampum beads were strung on threads. A string of wampum beads almost 2 meters long was worth about five British shillings or one U.S. dollar in colonial times. A string of that value had 360 white beads and 180 purple or black beads. It could be used for trading among Native Americans or with European-Americans.

Wampum belts were used both as money and to conduct official business between tribes.

But there was a problem with wampum. Like other kinds of money, it could be made "counterfeit." Counterfeit money is false money without any value. In the late 17th century, counterfeit wampum became a problem at the Dutch colony in Manhattan, where New York City is today. The colony had to make a law defining which wampum was good, poor, and worthless. "Manhattan wampum" was the best quality. There was also a less valuable kind of wampum. Counterfeit wampum had no value at all.

Wampum had other uses too. It could be worn on clothing, just as people today wear jewelry made of gold or silver. There were necklaces, belts, and bracelets made of wampum. A more important use was in official business between Native American tribes. Wampum meant that a message from one tribe to another was official. The messenger carried a belt made of wampum. Different kinds of wampum belts were used for different kinds of business.

Wampum belts were even used to ratify peace treaties. The Cherokee people, for example, had wampum belts that showed they had made peace with the Iroquois people❷.

Wampum beads were only one kind of beads that Native Americans made. They also made beads from many other materials, including turquoise, quartz, copper, and the teeth and bones of animals. These beads were used as money or worn on clothing. They had ceremonial uses as well. Large amounts of beads were often buried with the dead.

Reminders of the "age of wampum" and beads can be seen in the United States today. One kind of bead used in Virginia was called "Roanoke." Today, there is a city named Roanoke, Virginia!

❷ The Cherokee and the Iroquois were two of the largest Native American tribes in the eastern part of America.

◁》 Cherokee [tʃérəkìː]
◁》 Iroquois [írəkwɔi]
◁》 periwinkle [périwiŋkl]
◁》 quohog [kwɔ́ːhɔːɡ]
◁》 Roanoke [róuənðuk]
◁》 wampum [wɑ́mpəm]

📑 WORDS FOR BASIC ECONOMICS
✓ bead
✓ counterfeit
✓ material
✓ paper money
✓ ratify
✓ trade
✓ treaty
✓ tribe
✓ value

Questions

01 Look at the word **lining** in the passage. What do you think **lining** means in this context?

02 What was wampum made from? What other materials did the Native Americans use as money?

03 What diplomatic purpose did wampum serve for the Native Americans?

04 What can you infer from this passage about the Dutch colony at Manhattan? What kind of relationship did the Dutch have with Native Americans? Explain.

1.2 The 18th Century: The Trouble with Paper Money

People had little trust in the value of the Continental dollar.

❶ They did this by mixing the silver or gold with other, cheaper metals such as lead and copper.

doubtful.

One symbol of America is the "greenback," or United States dollar bill. It is paper money. It is easy to carry and is accepted around the world. Yet, the American government more than 200 years ago was deeply **skeptical** about paper money and preferred "hard" money – that is, gold and silver coins. Why did the government at that time disapprove of paper money? To understand, we have to go back more than 100 years before the American Revolution, to England around the year 1660.

England had no paper money before the mid-17th century. Money took the form of gold or silver coins. But the government "debased" the coins by reducing their gold or silver content❶, and kept the gold or silver that was removed.

— to make sth or sth lose its value —

When people saw what was happening, they refused to accept the debased coins because the coins were actually worth less than the original coins. Then, the courts (which were part of the government) simply said that the gold or silver content did not matter. The debased money, the courts said, was worth whatever the government said it was worth.

From there, it was only a short step to issuing paper money. Like debased coins, paper money had no value of its own. (Here it differed from gold and silver, which always kept their value.) But as in the case of debased coins, the government could simply say that the paper money was worth something.

Many people found this system convenient. Paper was easier to carry than metal coins. So, people accepted paper money and forgot that the paper itself was worthless. People just pretended that it was worth something, because the government said so. This made paper money even worse than debased coins, which at least had a little gold or silver in them.

Nonetheless, the United States government used paper money during the Revolutionary War. This money was called "Continental currency." After the war, however, Congress became worried. People no longer accepted Continental currency. It was considered worthless, because it was. So, Congress asked Thomas Jefferson for advice on what kind of currency the new country should use.

Jefferson told Congress that the American people already had a preferred currency: the Spanish dollar. Also known as a "piece of eight" because it was an eight-sided coin, it was made of gold or silver and was already in widespread use. Congress therefore made the Spanish dollar America's official currency.

But banks were still allowed to issue paper money. In principle, the paper money could be turned in to a bank in return for gold. But banks tended to issue more paper money than they had gold. That meant the banks did not have enough gold to support their paper money, and so the paper money was not worth what the banks said it was.

Jefferson opposed this practice. He feared the U.S. would be flooded with paper money, which would become as worthless as the old Continental currency. "I am an enemy to ... anything but coin," Jefferson wrote. The banks, however, wanted paper money. They profited from issuing it. They also had powerful friends in the government. So, getting rid of paper money would not be easy.

Thus began a long struggle in the U.S. over paper money versus real money, and banks' interests against everyone else's. The struggle continues to this day.

WORDS FOR BASIC ECONOMICS
- ✓ congress
- ✓ convenient
- ✓ currency
- ✓ debase
- ✓ disapprove
- ✓ hard money
- ✓ issue
- ✓ profit
- ✓ widespread
- ✓ worthless

Questions

01 Look at the word **skeptical** in the text. What do you think **skeptical** means in this context?

02 Why did people refuse to accept "debased" English coins?

03 What role did the courts play in the transition to paper money?

04 Why did Americans in Jefferson's time prefer the Spanish dollar?

1.3 The 18ᵗʰ Century: Decimal Coinage

America adopted a much simpler coin system based on decimals.

When the United States became independent from Britain, many things in America changed. One thing that changed greatly was the system of coins used. The British used an old, awkward system that was **derived** in part from ancient Rome. Britain's unit of money, the pound, was divided into 20 "shillings" or 240 "pence." There were many other subdivisions of British currency as well. Other European countries such as France, Germany, and Spain used different but still awkward systems for counting money.

There was a better way: the decimal system, arranged in units of 10. About 200 years before the American Revolution, Dutch mathematician Simon Stevin van Brugghe invented decimals to provide a more convenient system for counting than fractions. In decimals, the fraction 1/2 became 0.5, 1/4 became 0.25, and so on. Adding and subtracting decimals was easy.

American thinkers such as Thomas Jefferson knew about the decimal system, and Jefferson thought it should be used as the basis for a new U.S. currency. So, when the U.S. set up its unit of currency, the dollar, it used the decimal system. The dollar was divided into 10 smaller units called "dimes." (At first, "dime" was spelled "disme.") Each dime, in turn, was divided into 10 "cents" or "pennies." There was also a "half-dime" that was worth five cents. Today, we call it the "nickel."

It was easy to perform arithmetic with decimal coinage. 100 cents equaled 10 dimes. 10 dimes equaled one dollar. There was no need to struggle with fractions when using decimal coinage. By using decimals, the United States made a great advance in currency systems. Decimals made everything simple.

Half-dimes were the first U.S. coins issued, in 1792. President

George Washington, in a speech, took note of this modest start with a new currency. The government made only 1,500 half-dimes in this first batch❶. Jefferson gave many of them away as presents. In Jefferson's honor, the United States later put his image on the coin. Today, the "Jefferson nickel" is an everyday sight. George Washington had his image put on the quarter, or 25-cent coin.

❶ A *batch* means a certain number or amount of a product which is made at the same time.

Since 1792, the United States has issued coins in many different designs. Some have shown images of presidents (Abraham Lincoln, Franklin Roosevelt, Dwight Eisenhower) born long after the time of Jefferson and Washington. The decimal system, however, has remained unchanged. A dollar today is 100 cents, or 20 nickels, or 10 dimes, just as it always has been. Although an American may not have invented the decimal system, an American – Thomas Jefferson – put it to one of its most important uses, as the basis for counting a new nation's currency.

🔊 Dwight Eisenhower
[dwɑit áizənhàuər]
🔊 Simon Stevin van Brugghe
[sáimən stévən væn brúːɡə]

📑 **WORDS FOR BASIC ECONOMICS**

✓ arithmetic ⟶ ⟨handwritten⟩
✓ arrange
✓ coinage
✓ decimal
✓ derive
✓ divide
✓ fraction

Questions

01   Where did the British monetary system originate?

02   What problems did the British monetary system have?

03   What were the first coins issued in the United States?

04   What can you infer about the government's attitude towards the new half-dimes when they were first issued?

05   Look at the word **derived** in the passage. What do you think **derived** means in this context?

1.4 The 19ᵗʰ Century: Thorstein Veblen

Thorstein Veblen

❶ Johns Hopkins and Yale are two of the best universities in the United States. Top U.S. universities are often referred to as "Ivy League" schools.

❷ To *shake up* means to upset or disrupt the order of something.

One of the most famous Norwegian-Americans – and one of the most famous American economists and sociologists – was Thorstein Veblen. He lived from 1857 to 1929 and studied at Johns Hopkins University and Yale University❶. Veblen is remembered mainly for his famous book *The Theory of the Leisure Class*, published in 1899.

Veblen saw that a big "dichotomy," or conflict, existed between the traditional system of social status (that is, how highly a person ranks in society) and the technological basis of society (the tools that society needs in order to work). This concept is sometimes called the "Veblenian dichotomy" in Veblen's honor.

Veblen said this dichotomy was "ceremonial" and "instrumental." On the one hand, social status had a "ceremonial" basis that had its origins in history and led to differences in social status. On the other hand, social status also had an "instrumental" aspect that was related to technology and tended to create an entirely different system of status and power. These two aspects opposed each other. That is, the "instrumental" element tended to upset the "ceremonial" element. This created the "Veblenian dichotomy." It thus shook up❷ society from time to time, when someone with a really good new idea or invention came along.

Here is another way to look at Veblen's idea. Imagine a society has been controlled for a long time by a few rich and powerful families. Their great power and high status have their origin in history. Those families are rich and powerful because they always have been rich and powerful.

Now, imagine that someone of lesser wealth and status invents a new machine or process that makes him or her a lot of money and changes society greatly. Suddenly, the inventor has a much higher status than before, and may become as **influential** as the old, wealthy families. In other words, the people at the top face new competition. Then, the "instrumental" element has opposed the "ceremonial" element and upset the long-established order of status and social rank, as technology provides a way to climb the social ladder❸, so to speak.

to be socially or politically powerful

This has happened many times in American history. Inventors found that their work could make them and their families just as rich and powerful as anyone else. So, one did not have to be born into a wealthy, powerful family to become rich and powerful. Someone lower in rank, but with a good understanding of technology, could get the same result.

Veblen also studied and wrote about other subjects including the price system, higher education, and the history of the industrial revolution. The great economist died less than three months before one of the greatest economic events in 20th-century America: the crash of 1929, which started the Great Depression❹.

❸ To *climb the social ladder* means to increase one's status in society.

❹ This refers to the stock market crash of 1929, which started the Great Depression, a time of severe economic hardship in the U.S.

🔊 **Norwegian** [nɔːrwíːdʒən]
🔊 **Thorstein Veblen** [θɔ́ːrstain véblən]

📋 **WORDS FOR BASIC ECONOMICS**
✓ competition
✓ crash
✓ depression
✓ element
✓ influential
✓ oppose
✓ origin
✓ social status
✓ upset
✓ wealth

Questions

01 Briefly explain Veblen's theory in your own words.

02 Give an example of a rich and famous person who would represent the ceremonial side of Veblen's theory and another person who would represent the instrumental side of his theory.

03 Look at the word **influential** in the text. What do you think **influential** means in this context?

1.5 The 19th Century: The "Free Silver" Movement

William Jennings Bryan ran for president with the promise to promote silver currency.

❶ At the time, the U.S. dollar was based on the "gold standard." This meant that a dollar actually represented a certain amount of gold. The free silver movement wanted to change to a "silver standard."

Much of U.S. politics in the 19th century involved the question of silver coins. This issue reached its peak in the "free silver" movement of the late 1800s.

The expression "free silver" referred to a political movement that sought the unlimited use of silver coins. Free silver became a major issue after the "panic of 1873," in which a stock market crash led to an economic depression that hurt farmers in the southern and western U.S. badly. *-to increase in price or make sth increase in price.*

Farmers wanted to inflate the U.S. dollar (that is, increase the supply of money) so they could pay off their debts more easily. In other words, they wanted "cheap money." They thought silver money would work as well for that purpose as paper money because silver was worth much less than gold, and silver prices were falling at the time. Silver miners in the western U.S. also supported the free silver movement because it would help their industry❶.

Advocates of cheap money formed a political party, the "Greenback Party." By 1880, the "Greenbackers" were a powerful force in American politics. They hoped to win the presidency.

Congress saw that something had to be done. The political pressures were too great to ignore. At the same time, however, "free silver" had powerful opponents in the eastern U.S. The financial establishment – the banks – preferred gold to silver. The gold standard, as it was called, worked against farmers because it would not let them pay off their debts easily with cheap silver.

Bleo

Congress tried a compromise. In 1878, the Bland-Allison Act was passed. It allowed limited coinage of silver and set the ratio of silver to gold at 16 to 1. But this **measure** did not work, and Congress tried again in 1890. This time, Congress passed another

-the system or type of money used in a country.

compromise, the Sherman Silver Purchase Act. It allowed the government to buy more silver.

to engage in an operation planned to achieve a certain goal.

Yet even the Sherman Act was not enough for free silver's supporters. They were tired of compromises. Their unrest strengthened the Populist Party, which was formed in 1892 and campaigned for free silver and abundant paper money. The silver issue became even more intense after the Sherman Act was repealed following another "panic❷" in 1893.

Financial crisis

❷ *Panic* is often used to describe a financial crisis.

So, the two sides, gold versus silver, prepared for battle in the presidential election of 1896. On the one side were the Populists, in favor of free silver. On the other side were the financial interests in favor of gold and "sound money." Free silver's candidate was William Jennings Bryan. The candidate of gold and "sound money" was William McKinley.

Though Bryan spoke eloquently in favor of free silver, McKinley won the election. Soon afterward, the economy improved, and the "free silver" movement passed into history. Thereafter, the U.S. silver supply declined until the U.S. ceased making silver coins in the 1960s and sold its surplus silver in 1970.

📑 **WORDS FOR BASIC ECONOMICS**

✓ abundant
✓ decline
✓ financial
✓ inflate
✓ opponent
✓ panic
✓ peak
✓ repeal
✓ stock market
✓ strengthen
✓ supply
✓ surplus

Questions

01 Look at the word **measure** in the text. What do you think **measure** means in this context?

02 What was the objective of the free silver movement?

03 Why did farmers support free silver? What other supporters did free silver have? Who were its opponents?

04 What ended the free silver movement?

1.6   The 19th-20th Century: Oil and the U.S. Economy

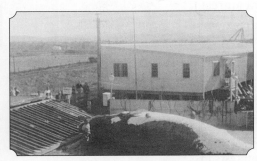
Whale oil was the dominant source of lamp oil in the 1800s.

In the 18th and early 19th centuries, oil from whales was very valuable in America. Whale oil was an important source of energy. Used in lamps, it burned with a very clean flame. So, "whaling," or hunting whales for their oil, was an important industry. Many ships took part in whaling, and the sale of whale oil made much money for businessmen in the early United States. Selling whale oil was profitable because it was very expensive. In the early 19th century, a liter of good whale oil cost about 50 cents. In modern currency, that is about 50 dollars! Not all whale oil was so valuable, but even cheaper whale oil was important as a lubricant, to keep machines running smoothly.

In the first half of the 19th century, the United States had a big whaling industry. By the late 1840s, the U.S. had more than 700 whaling ships. They brought in between 38 million and 57 million liters of whale oil per year. The whaling industry was also an important part of American culture. Herman Melville❶ wrote the most famous American novel, *Moby Dick*, about life on a whaling ship in the early 1800s. New Bedford, Massachusetts, was an especially important whaling town. In Melville's novel, the narrator, "Ishmael," visits New Bedford before he sails on the whaling ship *Pequod* in search of Moby Dick, the white whale.

But the United States was growing and becoming an industrial nation. Whale oil could not supply all its needs. So, after petroleum was discovered in the mid-1800s, America used increasing amounts of oil from the ground. The introduction of kerosene, known then as "coal oil," meant the end of the great whaling industry. Petroleum fuel was easier to make than whale oil, and much cheaper. The price of whale oil dropped in response, but whale oil still could not compete with petroleum. In 1895, for example, the best whale oil sold for about 10 cents per liter. Oil made from petroleum, on the

❶ Herman Melville is one of the most famous 19th-century American novelists. He wrote stories about ships and the sea.

other hand, was less than 2 cents per liter. Soon, the whaling industry was only history preserved in museums.

At the beginning of the 20th century, petroleum became America's major energy source.

The 20th century, then, was the century of petroleum and petroleum products in America. From kerosene-fueled lanterns to gasoline-fueled automobiles, the U.S. depended on petroleum for fuel and lubrication. A huge "petrochemical" industry also arose, to make oil into everything from drugs to dinner plates. By 1950, an America without cheap, abundant oil was hard to imagine.

For a hundred years, the American economy ran on petroleum, and no one wished to think about what would happen when the oil ran out. As the 21st century began, however, the world's oil supply had Americans worried. Was the world about to **exhaust** its oil? In that case, what would happen to the U.S. economy, which depended on oil for almost everything? There were no easy answers to that second question – or at least, no comforting answers.

🔊 Herman Melville [hɜ́ːrmən mélvil]
🔊 Ishmael [íʃmeil]
🔊 *Pequod* [píːkwɑd]

📖 **WORDS FOR BASIC ECONOMICS**

✓ compete
✓ currency
✓ depend
✓ exhaust
✓ lubricant
✓ preserve
✓ profitable
✓ valuable

Questions

01 What were the uses of whale oil?

02 How did the whaling industry affect American culture?

03 What brought about the end of the whaling industry?

04 What is the current energy problem in the U.S.?

05 Look at the word **exhaust** in the text. What do you think **exhaust** means in this context?

1.7 The 20th Century: What Started the Great Depression?

❶ The Great Depression was an extremely bad financial crisis. Jobs were difficult to find and many people lost their homes.

❷ *Boom* can be used to mean to grow or increase at a rapid pace.

❸ The Federal Reserve is the government agency that controls banking and economic issues in the U.S.

❹ An *interest rate* is the amount of extra money people must pay when they pay back a loan. Interest rates are partly determined by the Federal Reserve, a part of the government that controls banks.

The Great Depression❶ was the worst time in the lives of many Americans during the 20th century. After the stock market crashed in 1929, millions of Americans suddenly found themselves thrown into poverty without hope of getting out.

What brought on the Great Depression? It had many causes. In summary, however, this is what happened.

During the 1920s, the stock market boomed❷ in the U.S. People were optimistic about the future. They thought the government would keep the economy healthy, markets would keep growing, and the standard of living would keep rising. Ordinary people invested in the stock market, thinking they would get rich.

So, stocks went up and up. There seemed to be no end in sight. By September 1929, perhaps 40 percent of stock market value (that is, almost half) was purely imaginary. It existed only in people's dreams. When the stock market fell suddenly a few weeks later, on October 29, 1929, Americans learned the difference between imaginary wealth and real wealth. Stocks lost 10 percent of their value in a single day. That event was called "the crash."

The crash happened after the U.S. Federal Reserve❸ decided the stock market was getting out of control. The market looked like a "bubble": a rate of growth that could not continue for long. If the bubble burst, so to speak, it could hurt the economy badly.

So, the Federal Reserve increased interest rates❹ in 1928 and 1929 to "cool down" the market. It worked. The market cooled down. But what happened after that took the country by surprise.

The Federal Reserve's move slowed down the U.S. economy. A recession occurred. This was not what people expected. They had thought the good times would go on endlessly. As events demonstrated, they were wrong.

to make sb suddenly surprised or slightly shocked.

Startled, companies reduced production. Consumers bought less. Demand for products fell. So did prices. When prices began falling (a process called "deflation"), they kept on falling, because the initial drop in prices led to further deflation.

Soon, prices were falling by 10 percent per year. Investors stopped investing their money because they could not be sure of making more money when prices were falling. At the same time, banks were failing, and the world's monetary system was falling apart. In short, things went from bad to worse.

When the depression was at its worst, things looked hopeless. Workers were out of work because companies would not hire them. Companies would not hire workers because there was no market for the goods they made. And why was there no market? Workers had no money to buy things because companies would not hire them. Production per worker dropped by almost half. One out of every four American workers was unemployed.

Thus, an initial recession became the Great Depression. The bad times just kept going. Americans who had thought they were rich, or at least solid members of the middle class, now joined the ranks of the poor – **wiped out** by a bubble and an illusion of wealth. And below the merely poor were the poorest of the poor, who had to live in cardboard "homes❺" that washed away with the rain. Such housing was a good metaphor for pre-crash dreams of prosperity.

❺ Because they were very poor, they had to build their homes out of ordinary cardboard boxes. These "homes" provided very little shelter and did not last long.

📋 **WORDS FOR BASIC ECONOMICS**

✓ boom
✓ bubble
✓ consumer
✓ crash
✓ deflation
✓ demand
✓ depression
✓ interest rate
✓ invest
✓ monetary system
✓ prosperity
✓ recession
✓ unemployed

Questions

01 Why were Americans so optimistic about the stock market in the 1920s?

02 Why was it so difficult to stop the Great Depression? Describe the cycle of events that made it continue.

03 Look at the expression **wiped out** in the passage. What do you think **wiped out** means in this context?

1.8 The 20ᵗʰ Century: John Kenneth Galbraith

Born in Canada in 1908, John Kenneth Galbraith is one of the most **renowned** American economists of the 20ᵗʰ and early 21ˢᵗ century. He is famous for suggesting that government should help to manage a nation's economy. In his many books and articles, he is known for suggesting that the government should take an "activist" role in running a nation's economy, instead of leaving business alone. This view is opposed to more traditional thinking, in which government "interference" in the economy is considered a danger to be avoided.

In *American Capitalism*, published in 1952, Galbraith imagined that the U.S. economy of the future would be run by a combination of big business, organized labor, and government. The government in this case would be "activist," or actively involved in managing the economy. This system would be a change from the early 20ᵗʰ century, when big business dominated the economy, unions were relatively weak, and government played only a small role in running the nation's economy❶.

One of Galbraith's most famous works is *The New Industrial State*, published in 1967. In it, he pointed out that the model of perfect competition does not apply to many American industries❷. In another famous book, *The Affluent Society*, published in 1958, Galbraith argued that the United States, to be successful, would have to spend heavily on education and on projects such as roads. (*The Affluent Society* was a bestseller.) In 1990, Galbraith published a history of financial "bubbles❸" and irrational elements behind them. His other works include *Economics and the Public Purpose* (1973), *Money* (1975), and *The Age of Uncertainty* (1977).

Galbraith is said to have influenced U.S. government policies in the early 1960s, when *The Affluent Society* allegedly helped to bring about

John Kenneth Galbraith

❶ In the early 20th century, businesses held great power over their employees, and work conditions were often horrible as a result.

❷ The guiding theory behind the U.S. economy is capitalism. Capitalism says that competition between companies will automatically regulate business and that this works in the consumer's favor. This is the model of perfect competition.

❸ A *bubble* is an artificial sense of wealth in an industry. It appears there is more money and profit than there actually is. A good example would be the internet bubble of the 1990s when many people believed internet companies were more successful than they actually were.

the federal government's "war on poverty❹," a spending program that has been criticized for ineffectiveness. His critics include economist Milton Friedman, who saw Galbraith's work as a defense of extending government power. Galbraith also has been criticized for making America's industrial system appear much simpler than it really was.

Galbraith attended the University of Guelph (then Ontario Agricultural College) in Canada. He later earned his M.S. and Ph.D. degrees from the University of California in Berkeley. He was head of the Office of Price Administration in World War II and joined the faculty of Harvard University in 1949. He served as U.S. ambassador to India from 1961 to 1963.

Though strongly criticized by more conservative economists such as Friedman, Galbraith is known for writing popular, easily understandable books about economics. He also is a well-known critic of economic forecasting.

❹ The war on poverty was a series of government funded social programs to improve the lives of poor people.

◁) Guelph [gwɛlf]
◁) John Kenneth Galbraith [dʒɑn kéniθ gǽlbreiθ]
◁) Milton Friedman [mílten fríːdmən]

📑 **WORDS FOR BASIC ECONOMICS**
✓ big business
✓ bubble
✓ capitalism
✓ conservative
✓ criticize
✓ dominate
✓ financial
✓ ineffectiveness
✓ interference
✓ perfect competition
✓ renowned
✓ union

Questions

01 Look at the word **renowned** in the text. What do you think **renowned** means in this context?

02 What did Galbraith believe about the role of government in business?

03 What effects did Galbraith's beliefs have on government policy?

04 What problems did Galbraith's critics find in his ideas? Explain.

1.9 The 20th Century: Supply-Side Economics

Supply-side economics places great emphasis on production.

O nly rarely does a school of economic thought become a household word❶. That happened in the U.S. during the 1980s, however, as the administration of President Ronald Reagan supported "supply-side" economics as a way to help America strengthen its economy.

Supply-side economics emerged in the 1970s. It was based on the idea that people and their societies get rich by making things – that is, increasing their supply. Because it emphasized increasing supply, this way of thinking was called "supply-side economics."

❶ The term *household word* describes something that is well known across society.

Here is how it was supposed to work. In an industrial country, for example, people would get rich by making things like cars, computers, or furniture. The supply of those things would increase. Other people would buy them. Money then would flow to the maker of the products, who would get richer. That wealth, in turn, would spread to the rest of society as the wealthy person spent it on a house, a boat, or whatever. Thus, society as a whole would benefit from increasing supply.

How could government encourage people to make things and build wealth? According to supply-side thought, it was important to cut taxes and make it easier to do business. Then, businesses would find it easier to do their work, make things, increase supply, and create wealth.

Of course, there was more to supply-side economics than this. But these basic principles – cutting taxes and helping business – appealed to many people in the United States, including President

Ronald Reagan and his administration during the 1980s.

Reagan's fiscal policies were based in part on supply-side thinking. The Reagan administration promoted supply-side policies as a way to help the economy get out of the economic **doldrums** of the 1970s, when bad times started around 1973 with a sharp rise in oil prices, then continued for the rest of the decade.

To help America recover from those economic bad times, the Reagan administration and Congress reduced taxes and business regulations in the early 1980s. At the same time, all Americans received income tax cuts. People then had more money to spend, and the U.S. economy boomed for seven years. That effect was seen as a victory for the "supply-siders."

❷ To *go down in history* means to be remembered forever.

Supply-side policy had critics who thought it increased the gap in income between the rich and poor. Other critics said tax cuts increased the federal deficit – the difference between what the government spent and what it collected in taxes.

But even critics acknowledge that Reagan's "supply-side revolution" of the 1980s accompanied a time of great prosperity. For that reason alone, supply-side economics would go down in U.S. history❷ as one of the most important schools in 20th-century economic thought.

📋 **WORDS FOR BASIC ECONOMICS**

✓ appeal
✓ benefit
✓ boom
✓ decade
✓ deficit
✓ emerge
✓ encourage
✓ promote
✓ reduce
✓ regulation
✓ supply
✓ support
✓ tax

Questions

01 How was supply-side economics supposed to help poor and middle class people? Explain.

02 What did the Reagan administration do to support supply-side economics?

03 To what extent was supply-side economics successful in the U.S.? What problems did it cause? Explain.

04 Look at the word **doldrums** in the passage. What do you think **doldrums** means in this context?

SOCIAL SCIENCES II

Political Science

2.1 The 18th Century: Thomas Jefferson and the Declaration of Independe

❶ Jefferson was one of the most influential Americans in early U.S. history and 3rd president of the U.S.

The most famous achievement of Thomas Jefferson's❶ life was the writing of the Declaration of Independence in 1776. That document informed the British government of King George III that the British colonies in America would no longer be subject to the king. Instead, they would form an independent country.

Originally, Jefferson had not planned to write the Declaration of Independence. He really wanted to work on a constitution for his state, Virginia. The Continental Congress❷, however, made Jefferson one member of a five-person committee assigned to produce a draft of the Declaration of Independence. Other members of the committee were John Adams of Massachusetts, Benjamin Franklin of Pennsylvania, Robert Livingston of New York, and Roger Sherman of Connecticut. The committee assigned Jefferson to write the draft.

The Declaration of Independence is one of the most important documents in U.S. history.

❷ The Continental Congress served as the preliminary government for the U.S. before the Constitution was completed.

He drew on many sources for ideas and information, including the Virginia Declaration of Rights, written by George Mason and Thomas Lee. The Virginia Declaration of Rights used much of the same language and many of the same ideas that Jefferson used to write the Declaration of Independence. Jefferson also had written several drafts of a constitution for Virginia, and he used those drafts in writing the Declaration of Independence as well.

Jefferson made many changes in his draft of the Declaration of Independence. A fragment of the first draft survives. It is heavily edited and includes many changes. When a rough draft was ready, Jefferson presented it to the committee and especially to John Adams and Benjamin Franklin. This original rough draft is now in the Library of Congress in Washington, D.C. In the margins of the draft, Jefferson later wrote changes that Franklin and Adams recommended.

The committee then submitted its work to Congress, which made further changes in the document. At last, the final version was ready. John Hancock, president of the Continental Congress, had the work sent to George Washington❸, who had the document read to his soldiers in New York City. After hearing the Declaration of Independence read, the soldiers were so excited that they tore down a statue of King George III.

❸ At the time, Washington was the commander of the Continental Army and later became the first president of the U.S.

Jefferson was not completely pleased with the final version. He thought Congress had damaged his work. To his friend Richard Henry Lee, Jefferson wrote later, "I wish ... that the manuscript had not been mangled❹ as it is." Jefferson complained that "change [was] unhappily applied." Still, he thought that the document on the whole was good.

❹ *Mangled* means ruined or damaged.

To write the Declaration of Independence, Jefferson used what was, for that time, high technology. He wrote the work on a small, portable "lap desk" that he designed and had built by a cabinet maker in Philadelphia. So, Jefferson wrote his famous document on the 18ᵗʰ-century **equivalent** of a laptop computer! The desk is kept now in the Smithsonian Institution in Washington.

📖 **WORDS FOR POLITICAL SCIENCE**

✓ congress
✓ constitution
✓ document
✓ draft
✓ equivalent
✓ independent
✓ survive

Political Science

Questions

01 Why didn't Jefferson want to work on the Declaration of Independence? What did he really want to do?

02 What sources did Jefferson use to help him write the Declaration of Independence?

03 How many drafts did the Declaration of Independence go through before it was completed? Describe the process in your own words.

04 Look at the word **equivalent** in the passage. What do you think **equivalent** means in this context?

2.2   The 18ᵗʰ Century: Separation of Powers

The writers of the U.S. Constitution did not want the government of their new nation to have too much power. They had just finished fighting a war against England's powerful king and did not wish to give the United States a government where one person or branch of government could get too much power.

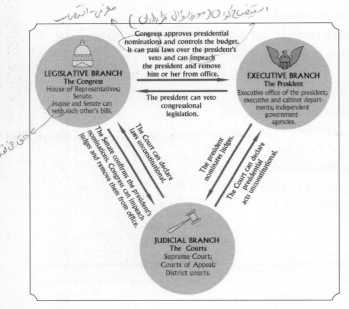

Congress approves presidential nominations and controls the budget. It can pass laws over the president's veto and can impeach the president and remove him or her from office.

LEGISLATIVE BRANCH
The Congress
House of Representatives;
Senate.
House and Senate can veto each other's bills.

The president can veto congressional legislation.

EXECUTIVE BRANCH
The President
Executive office of the president; executive and cabinet departments; independent government agencies.

The Senate confirms the president's nominations. Congress can impeach judges and remove them from office.

The Court can declare laws unconstitutional.

The president nominates judges.

The Court can declare presidential acts unconstitutional.

JUDICIAL BRANCH
The Courts
Supreme Court;
Courts of Appeal;
District courts.

How did the Constitution's authors do this? They wrote the Constitution to allow for "separation of powers." This meant "splitting up" government powers among several branches, so that no one branch could get too much power.

Separation of powers was not a new idea then. In fact, the ancient Greeks discussed it long before. But during the 17ᵗʰ and 18ᵗʰ centuries, European thinkers looked at the idea again. The French thinker Montesquieu divided government into three branches, or "powers." One was the legislative branch, which made laws. The second was the executive branch, which enforced the laws. The third was the judicial branch, which interpreted laws.

The writers of the U.S. Constitution used this three-branch system. They divided the U.S. government into three branches. The legislative branch was Congress, which made laws. The executive branch included the president and other executives, who enforced the laws. (Another name for the president is the "chief executive.") The judicial branch, which included the Supreme Court and lower courts, interpreted the laws.

These three branches were supposed to keep one another in check❶. That is, if one branch started to get too powerful, the other branches would restrain it. The result was a complex system of "checks and balances." Power was balanced, so to speak, among the three branches.

How did checks and balances work? Here is an example. Congress had the power to make laws, but its power was not total. The other branches could oppose laws that they thought were unfair. The president had the power to veto a law (in other words, refuse to approve it) if he thought it was wrong. Also, the judicial branch could decide whether or not a law was "constitutional," or in keeping with the Constitution. If the court declared a law "unconstitutional," then it could not be enforced.

The Constitution imposed similar checks and balances on all three branches of government. In principle, checks and balances would prevent any one branch of government – legislative, executive, or judicial – from getting too much power. If that happened, the other branches would "check," or restrain, its growth.

The Constitution's system of separation of powers and checks and balances was not perfect. It worked well enough, however, to keep the young United States from becoming a **tyranny**.

❶ To *keep in check* means to prevent someone or something from becoming too powerful, or to control.

🔊 Montesquieu [mántəskjùː]

📋 **WORDS FOR POLITICAL SCIENCE**

✓ checks and balances
✓ declare
✓ enforce
✓ executive branch
✓ impose
✓ interpret
✓ judicial branch
✓ legislative branch
✓ oppose
✓ separation of powers
✓ unconstitutional
✓ unfair

Political Science

Questions

01   What were the writers of the U.S. Constitution afraid of? Explain.

02   Where did the Americans get the idea of separation of powers?

03   Name the three branches of government created by separation of powers and explain the role of each branch in your own words.

04   Look at the word **tyranny** in the passage. What do you think **tyranny** means in this context?

2.3   The 18ᵗʰ-20ᵗʰ Century: The Two-Party System

The two-party system has always dominated American politics.

ratify = اسوله تمام شده و مشروع غير قانوني /to ratify

A major feature of American politics is its "two-party system." There are only two major political parties. Traditionally, they have offered voters a choice of policies on important issues ranging from currency to foreign wars. Although there have been many other, smaller political parties in American history, the two-party system has provided the basis for elections and for U.S. politics in general. Voters appear to prefer the "either-or" choice❶ that a two-party system provides.

confirmation

America's two-party system began more than 200 years ago. The issue that created them was the ratification of the U.S. Constitution. There were two parties then: the Federalists and the Anti-federalists. The Federalists wanted a strong central government, wished to limit the rights of states, and thought a Bill of Rights in the Constitution was not needed. The Anti-federalists, on the other hand, were **wary** of a strong central government. They wanted states to have greater authority and thought the Constitution had to include a Bill of Rights❷. There were other differences, too. The Federalists thought the United States should be a big republic, whereas the Anti-federalists thought just the opposite; they believed that a small republic would protect citizens' rights better.

To be careful or cautious about sth

❶ *Either-or choice* means a choice of only one out of two options: either A or B, but not both.

❷ The Bill of Rights is the section of the Constitution which guarantees individual freedoms, like freedom of speech and freedom of religion.

Political parties came and went and changed names over the years, but the basic two-party system remained, mainly because of the way elections in the U.S. operate. Representatives to Congress and state legislatures are elected in districts where the candidate who gets the most votes becomes that district's sole representative. As only one winner is possible in each district, there tend to be only two parties, so that candidates can have the greatest possible chance of winning elections.

Today, the two major parties are the Republicans and the

Democrats. Nearly every elected official in the state and federal governments is either a Democrat or a Republican. Of course, it is possible for third parties to form and take part in elections, and many third parties (such as the Reform Party, the Populist Party, the American Independent Party, and the Green Party) have done so. It is difficult for third parties to win elections in the U.S., however, because the two-party system is so strong, and because third parties often merge with one of the two main parties during election campaigns, thus leaving the two-party system still in control.

The two major parties have animals as symbols. The Democrats are symbolized by a donkey, and the Republicans are symbolized by an elephant. This symbolism dates from the 19th century, when famous American cartoonist Thomas Nast used those two animals to depict the two parties. In this way, Nast added yet another tradition to the American two-party system.

to represent in a picture or sculpture

📑 WORDS FOR POLITICAL SCIENCE

- ✓ candidate
- ✓ depict
- ✓ district
- ✓ election
- ✓ legislature
- ✓ merge
- ✓ policy
- ✓ ratification
- ✓ representative
- ✓ republic

Questions

01 Why do Americans prefer the two-party system?

02 What event gave rise to the two-party system?

03 Explain the goals of the Federalists and the Anti-federalists.

04 Look at the word **wary** in the passage. What do you think **wary** means in this context?

05 Why is it difficult for third parties to gain power in the U.S. political system?

2.4 The 18th-20th Century: Who Elects a President?

Many people do not realize that the U.S. president is not directly elected by the people.

Many American voters are surprised to learn that their votes do not elect a president of the U.S. directly. Instead, the president is elected by a relatively tiny group called the Electoral College. It is made up of representatives, called "electors," from each of the 50 U.S. states. The electors are the people who actually select the winner in presidential elections.

"But the vote is supposed to reflect the will of the people," you may say. "Why are voters not allowed to elect a president directly? Why does a small group of people in the Electoral College choose the president instead?"

To answer those questions, we must look back to the 18th century, when the United States had just won its independence from Britain. The U.S. then was very different from the nation we know today. It was a string of small, weak states along the Atlantic coast of North America. Communications among the states were poor, so that a "national campaign" in the modern sense was impossible.

For these and other reasons, the makers of the U.S. Constitution devised a different way of electing a president. Because they had great respect for the ancient Romans, they adopted a system much like one used to vote on proposals presented by the Senate in Rome. That system was called the "Centurial College." The **framers** of the U.S. Constitution thought a similar system would work in choosing their president. That is how the American Electoral College began. Each state would appoint electors to the Electoral College, which then would choose the president and vice-president. This is still the system used today.

For this reason, direct popular vote does not determine who becomes president. In fact, it is possible for a candidate to win a

to form, plan, or arrange in the mind

writers or makers.

majority vote from the people and still lose the election in the Electoral College. That happened to Samuel Tilden in the election of 1876. He won more than half the popular vote but lost the vote in the Electoral College. Then, his opponent, Rutherford B. Hayes, was elected president.

The Electoral College has not always worked smoothly. In 1800, for example, it had trouble deciding who would be president. There were two candidates: Thomas Jefferson and Aaron Burr. At first, each received an equal number of votes. There was no clear winner. The House of Representatives then had to decide who would be president. It took the House of Representatives 36 tries to select Jefferson as the winner. To avoid having such a problem again, Congress added the 12th Amendment❶ to the Constitution to change the way the Electoral College cast its votes.

Should there be an electoral college at all? Some Americans say yes. Others say no. But the Electoral College has existed for more than two hundred years, so it is likely to last at least a little while longer.

❶ An *amendment* is an official change made to the U.S. Constitution.

🔊 **Aaron Burr** [ɛ́ərən bəːr]
🔊 **Rutherford B. Hayes** [rʌ́ðərfərd biː heiz]
🔊 **Samuel Tilden** [sǽmjuəl tíldən]

Political Science

📋 **WORDS FOR POLITICAL SCIENCE**

✓ adopt
✓ amendment
✓ appoint
✓ determine
✓ devise
✓ election
✓ independence
✓ majority
✓ senate

Q u e s t i o n s

01 In your own words, explain how the presidential election works in the United States.

02 Look at the word **framers** in the passage. What do you think **framers** means in this context?

03 Where did the Americans get the idea of an electoral college?

04 Give one historical example of a problem caused by the Electoral College.

2.5 The 18ᵗʰ-21ˢᵗ Century: Who Are "We the People"?

The concept of whom America was built for has changed greatly over the years.

❶ This came from the colonial era, when the definition of a citizen did not include non-whites, women, or people who did not own property.

The U.S. Constitution starts with the words "We the people ..." The Constitution has made that expression famous. When Americans want to refer to themselves as a nation, they say, "We the people ..." For centuries, Americans have spoken those words proudly. The words sound impressive. But what do they mean, exactly? To whom does that famous expression actually refer? "We the people," on close examination, turns out to have an **elusive** meaning. It is hard to say just what it means.

When the Constitution was written, did its authors speak for all the people in the newly formed United States? That was not the case. They spoke primarily for white, male owners of property❶. Not everyone was in that category. So, for whom precisely did the Constitution speak?

The young United States still had slaves of African descent. They were considered property. If the Constitution's reference to "the people" included them, then there was no clear indication that it did so. Were women considered part of "the people" in that document? One might say yes or no. Though women represented half of the adult population, women could not vote in American elections when the Constitution was written. They would not be able to vote until the early 20ᵗʰ century. Were they part of "the people" as mentioned in the Constitution?

Consider also the Native Americans, who had lived in America since long before the first Europeans arrived there. Native Americans certainly were not considered part of the people of the United States when the Constitution was written. On the contrary, they were considered savages, and many of the "American people" wished to see these original Americans killed. The natives were hardly considered "people" at all.

The point is this. "We the people" sounded inclusive, as if it meant everyone in the United States. But that expression was, and still is, strangely hard to define.

Although the commonly accepted definition of "the people" has expanded greatly over the last 200 years, many groups and individuals in the United States, in effect, remain outside it. They do not enjoy all the same rights and protections that the Constitution supposedly promises to "the people" of the U.S.❷

Does this mean the Constitution is meaningless? Certainly, it does not. Still, the uncertainty over the exact meaning of those three words raises some serious questions about equal rights under law, and about the whole concept of the American nation. When Americans say, "We the people," perhaps they should stop to think: "Who are 'we'?"

❷   Today, there are many illegal immigrants and foreigners living in the U.S. who do not have all of the rights guaranteed by the Constitution.

Political Science

📰 **WORDS FOR POLITICAL SCIENCE**

✓ constitution ✓   قانون اساسی
✓ definition
✓ descent
✓ elusive ✓   مبهم
✓ expand
✓ represent

Questions

01   Look at the word **elusive** in the passage. What do you think **elusive** means in this context?

02   What inaccurate assumption do modern Americans make about the words "We the people"? In what ways is it inaccurate?

2.6 The 19th Century: The Rise and Fall of Populism

UNITED WE STAND, DIVIDED WE FALL.
The Combined Forces of United Labor will Prove Invincible in their Onslaught

A poster for the People's Party

❶ The 19th century was a time of almost unlimited power for the rich, especially business owners. At that time, there were few unions, so workers had very little power to protect their rights or improve their work conditions. In addition, a small number of businessmen controlled virtually all business in America through powerful monopolies. These "barons" had great influence in the government.

American society has always had a tension between ordinary Americans and the rich and powerful minority at the top. In particular, many Americans have been suspicious of banks and bankers and have tried to limit their influence on the rest of society. This motive led to the rise of a new political movement called "populism" in America during the late 19th century. The name "populism" meant something like "politics for the benefit of the people," not merely for the benefit of a few wealthy people.

Populism was meant to represent ordinary people, as opposed to "big money" – what the populists called "concentrated capital." When politicians today claim to speak on behalf of the "average American" or "the little people," they are using the language of populism.

In the 19th century, businesses and banks were thought to have too much power. Their influence was seen as a threat to democracy in America. They had so much power in the U.S. congress and in state legislatures that lawmakers were seen only as the servants of the wealthy❶.

To oppose that influence, populism arose late in the 1800s. Populists wanted big changes in American society. They wanted to limit the power of banks and big business. Populists favored farmers and worked to make conditions better for them. Populists also wanted sweeping changes in the U.S. economy, such as "cheap money" that would let farmers pay off their debts more easily. The principle of "cheap money" was expressed in the "free silver" movement, which wanted unlimited use of silver money.

Populism had a political organization called the People's Party. At first, it was a success. In the early 1890s, it won much support from Americans because populists stood for what many ordinary people wanted: a louder voice in how the nation was run.

But several things worked against populism. It had powerful opponents. The rich had great resources and used them to attack populism and its supporters. Also, some populists used such strong language that they seemed "alarmist," or too extreme in their views. Populism's enemies made good use of such "extremists" to **discredit** populists and their movement.

Finally, the populists lost much of their strength in 1896, when they joined the Democrats to support William Jennings Bryan in the presidential election that year. When they joined the Democrats, the populists no longer seemed to have a clear voice or identity. Bryan lost the election. Soon afterward, the populists faded away. As a political party, the populists rose and fell in only a few years.

Even so, populism had a lasting effect on politics in America. The appeal of populism was powerful, and still is powerful, whenever large numbers of ordinary Americans see "the rich" as too powerful. Then, politicians who use populist language find that people listen.

🔊 William Jennings Bryan
[wíljəm dʒénɪŋz bráiən]

📖 **WORDS FOR POLITICAL SCIENCE**

✓ benefit
✓ democracy
✓ discredit
✓ influence
✓ lawmaker
✓ minority
✓ opponent
✓ supporter
✓ suspicious
✓ tension

Political Science

Questions

01   Look at the word **discredit** in the text. What do you think **discredit** means in this context?

02   What were the goals of the populists? Explain in your own words.

03   What kinds of people supported the populist movement? What were their motivations?

04   What hurt the populists and led to their fall? Explain.

2.7   The 19th Century: **Disputed Elections**

The 1876 election very nearly resulted in a second civil war.

❶ This dispute involved the state of Florida, where Bush's brother was governor. This fact made many people suspicious of the election results in Florida and added to the controversy.

❷ The occupation of the South by federal troops caused great anger in the South.

The American presidential election of 2000 was "disputed." That is, it was not clear for a time which candidate – George W. Bush or Albert Gore – had won the election❶. This disputed election had the world's attention for several weeks. But it was only the most recent in a series of disputed presidential elections in the U.S. More than 100 years earlier, just after the War Between the States, another disputed election came close to tearing the United States apart and starting a second civil war.

In the election of 1876, the two presidential candidates were Rutherford B. Hayes (a Republican) and Samuel Tilden (a Democrat). At first, Tilden appeared to have won the majority of the popular vote, and Hayes was almost ready to give up. Then, however, the Republicans learned that the Democrats were not sure about the situation in the Electoral College, the institution that actually elects the president. The president really is not chosen by popular vote. Each state appoints "electors" to the Electoral College, which then chooses the president.

The votes of three states – Florida, South Carolina, and Louisiana – in the Electoral College were uncertain, because each party there said the other had cheated in the election. Democrats, for example, were accused of keeping African-Americans from voting, whereas Republicans were thought to have thrown out many votes made by Democrats. It was hard to avoid suspecting fraud, especially because Florida, South Carolina and Louisiana were former members of the Confederacy (what the Southern states had called themselves during the war) and, in 1876, were still occupied by Northern troops❷.

Congress knew something had to be done quickly. The country

could not run for long without an elected president. Besides, Democrats warned they would use violence to put Tilden in office. That was a frightening threat. The United States had just fought one horrible civil war, from 1861 to 1865. Was a second civil war about to start only 11 years after the first one ended?

violence which results in loss of life

Afraid of new **bloodshed**, Congress set up a 15-man commission to resolve the disputed election. In secret, the Republican and Democrats reached a deal. If the Democrats would agree that Hayes (the Republican) had won the election, then Hayes, as president, would remove all Northern troops from the Southern states. The commission gave the Electoral College votes of Florida, South Carolina, and Louisiana to Hayes, and the Republicans won the election by only one electoral vote: 185 to 184. The next day – March 3, 1877 – Hayes became president.

🔊 Rutherford B. Hayes
　　[rʌðərfərd biː heiz]

🔊 Samuel Tilden
　　[sæmjuəl tíldən]

"Fraud!" cried many Democrats. But Hayes acted swiftly to remove Northern troops from the South, and Tilden's supporters accepted Hayes as the new president. One supporter of Tilden said, "I prefer ... Hayes' administration to four years of civil war." That is how the United States avoided a second civil war in the late 19th century.

📋 **WORDS FOR POLITICAL SCIENCE**

✓ accuse
✓ candidate
✓ dispute
✓ fraud
✓ occupy
✓ resolve
✓ threat
✓ violence

Political Science

Questions

01 Look at the word **bloodshed** in the text. What do you think **bloodshed** means in this context?

02 In your own words, explain what caused the dispute about the 1876 election?

03 Why was it important for the U.S. to resolve that dispute?

04 How was the dispute in the 1876 election resolved?

2.8 The 19th-21st Century: Positive versus Negative Politics

A cartoonist made fun of the Know-nothing party.

As a rule, Americans favor "positive" over "negative" political campaigns. That is, voters prefer a candidate who is in favor of something to another candidate who is merely against something.

There are many reasons for this preference. One reason is that voters may suspect a negative candidate has something to hide and is using negative politics to hide it. Also, a positive campaign tends to be stronger and more successful than a negative campaign because it is more effective to be for something than merely against something. A positive campaign usually projects an image of success, confidence, and optimism: three qualities that Americans like to see in elected officials.

Nonetheless, negativity has figured prominently in American politics from time to time, especially in times of social crisis. A good example of a negative political movement in the 19th century was the American Party, also known as the "Know-nothings." Here is how that strange name originated.

Many Americans in the early 19th century were Protestants by religion. They became frightened when large numbers of poor Roman Catholics from Europe – notably Irish and Germans – immigrated to the United States during the 1840s. The American Protestants feared that they would lose their dominant position in society. Therefore, in 1854, they formed a secret society in opposition to Roman Catholicism and pledged to vote only for Protestant candidates who were born in the United States. When asked about the political views of their group, members of the American Party would reply, "I know nothing." So, the party became known as the "Know-nothings."

The American Party became powerful, but only for a very short time. Its brief career shows how third parties in the U.S., especially those with a basically negative position, do not last long. This is partly because negative campaigns are **born of** fear, and fears tend to be short-lived.

be born of = created by or caused by.

In the 20th and 21st centuries, certain issues have been used effectively in negative politics, such as communism, crime, immigration, and student protest❶. Sometimes, candidates with negative campaigns have succeeded in making their opponents look weak, corrupt, or unpatriotic because of the opponents' stand on some very sensitive issue❷. Also, negative campaigns often have focused successfully on an opposing candidate's personal life. Such negative campaigns have made opponents look dishonest, cowardly, or immoral.

When a candidate has a definite weakness, negative politics can cost him or her an election. In general, however, negative politics can be so dangerous to its user that many candidates prefer not to use it. The positive approach is safer!

❶ Candidates have been able to win elections by simply being against these things, without presenting a positive alternative or any solution to social problems.

❷ A good example of this would be the 1950s, when many politicians attacked their opponents for not taking a strong enough stand against communism, and therefore being unpatriotic.

Political Science

🗐 **WORDS FOR POLITICAL SCIENCE**

✓ communism
✓ corrupt
✓ dominant
✓ effective
✓ immigrate
✓ pledge
✓ preference
✓ protest

Questions

01 Look at the expression **born of** in the passage. What do you think **born of** means in this context?

02 In your own words, explain the concept of negative politics.

03 Explain how the "Know-nothing" movement was an example of negative politics.

04 What is the great weakness of negative politics? Summarize that weakness in one sentence.

2.9 The 20th Century: Was Roosevelt's "New Deal" a Good Idea?

A major part of the New Deal was the creation of jobs for unemployed Americans.

❶ The Works Progress Administration, or the WPA, put unemployed Americans to work building roads, post offices, schools and other public facilities in order to reduce unemployment.

Faced with a nation devastated by poverty and unemployment during the Great Depression, President Franklin Roosevelt in 1932 promised "a new deal for the American people." His programs came to be known as the New Deal, because they were presented as an attempt to make life fairer for ordinary Americans and to help the United States recover from the Great Depression.

The New Deal involved many government programs to put the unemployed to work. One of these was the Works Progress Administration❶, a job program. The National Recovery Administration was supposed to stabilize wages and prices. The New Deal as a whole was seen as an effort to help the ordinary American, give greater power to labor unions, and reduce the power of big business in American society. The New Deal also established Social Security, a government-operated system of old-age pensions.

Was the New Deal a success? Not everyone thought so at the time, and not everyone thinks so now. On the contrary, Roosevelt's New Deal is widely seen today as a failure, on the whole. It did not do many things it was supposed to do.

The New Deal did not, for example, end the Great Depression. Only America's entry into World War II ended it, as the country **mobilized** for the fight against Japan, Germany, and Italy. Also, the New Deal did little or nothing to help the poor at the expense of the wealthy. The rich remained rich and the poor remained poor despite the New Deal. Unions gained some power under the New Deal, but big business remained strong.

The action of preparing for sth.

If the New Deal was a failure, then why did it fail? One explanation is that there was no single set of principles to guide it. According to this viewpoint, the New Deal tried to do too many things at once (make government more efficient, put the unemployed to work, end the Great Depression, stabilize the economy, et cetera) and, in the end, did none of them very well.

Regardless, the New Deal had a strong impact on American society. It led to widespread support for a stronger federal government and for government programs that redistributed income, such as Social Security, which took money from young, working Americans and gave it to older people.

The New Deal also produced the idea of an "activist" government that took an active part in managing the nation's economy and changing society. Activist government became a powerful force in American life during and after the Roosevelt years. When the administrations of Presidents John F. Kennedy and Lyndon Johnson tried to eliminate poverty in the U.S. during the 1960s through the federal "war on poverty❷," they were acting on principles laid down by Roosevelt's New Deal long before.

Yet an important question remained: how "activist" could the government afford to be? That question would be argued, pro and con, long after Roosevelt's death in 1945.

❷ This was another group of expensive, yet largely ineffective social programs designed to reduce the differences between the rich and poor in America.

📋 **WORDS FOR POLITICAL SCIENCE**

✓ efficient
✓ establish
✓ impact
✓ involve
✓ labor union
✓ mobilize
✓ reduce
✓ stabilize
✓ unemployment

Political **Science**

Questions

01 Explain the New Deal in your own words.

02 What caused the New Deal to fail?

03 Look at the word **mobilized** in the passage. What do you think **mobilized** means in this context?

04 What lasting effects did the New Deal have on American society?

2.10 The 20th Century: When Are "Rights" Wrong?

American society was based on the concept of "rights." These are freedoms or privileges granted by law to everyone. The Declaration of Independence, for example, lists the rights to "life, liberty, and the pursuit of happiness." Americans wanted to have certain rights guaranteed by law, such as the right to freedom of speech❶.

❶ Such freedoms are guaranteed by the Bill of Rights.

But when are "rights" wrong? That is, when do they go too far? That happens when one person's "right" interferes with someone else's rights. As humorist Will Rogers said, "Your freedom to swing your fists ends where my nose begins."

For example, someone has a right to free speech. But if he or she uses that freedom to spread lies that hurt or **endanger** others, the right of free speech no longer applies in that case. As one famous judge wrote, freedom of speech does not include the freedom to shout "Fire!" in a crowded theater.

Americans have had many arguments about rights. When some groups claimed "rights," other groups complained that those "rights" interfered with their rights. Here are some examples of such conflicts.

Someone has a right to build a home on his own land. But does he have a right to build an ugly home if it makes his neighbors' homes less valuable?

A company has a right to do business. But does a company have a "right" to operate a smelly factory near people's homes and make their lives unpleasant?

Freedom of the press is a right. But does a publisher have a "right" to publish books or magazines that make many people upset or angry?

The list goes on and on. Do children have a right to education? Do people have a right to housing? Do the poor have the right to receive an income at someone else's expense, even if they do no work? Do animals like cattle and chickens have rights that should govern how humans treat them? And should a corporation – that is, a business institution – have the same rights as a human being?

By the late 20th century, so many different groups were claiming "rights" for themselves that Americans had to stop and consider what a right really was – and what a "right" should mean. Many people appeared to think they had a "right" to whatever they wanted. They thought mere wishes had the same status as rights.

Of course, there is a difference between rights and desires. Person A does not necessarily have a right to something he or she wants, at the expense of person B. To take an imaginary case, suppose that you want to build a swimming pool in your yard but do not have enough money to do so. Then, your neighbor is not obligated to pay for your pool. Your wish does not equal a right.

Yet, not every case is as clear as that one. So, American lawmakers and courts in the late 20th century often had to address the difficult problem of rights – specifically, where rights began and ended. To make matters worse, strong emotions and huge amounts of money were involved ... and there appeared to be no end to claims of new "rights." Where would it all end?

📑 **Words for Political Science**

✓ claim
✓ concept
✓ conflict
✓ endanger
✓ expense
✓ freedom
✓ grant
✓ guarantee
✓ interfere
✓ privilege
✓ pursuit

Questions

01 The author uses a quote by Will Rogers to introduce the conflict of rights. Explain how this quote illustrates this conflict.

02 Look at the word **endanger** in the passage. What do you think **endanger** means in this context?

2.11 The 20th Century: The Lobbying Industry

"Money talks" in the lobbying industry.

One of the biggest industries in Washington, D.C. is "lobbying." In lobbying, groups with special interests try to persuade Congress to write laws that favor them. Such a group is called a "lobby," and its members are called "lobbyists." They spend much money every year trying to get the attention of lawmakers and influence the making of laws.

Lobbies may be anything from women's groups to big corporations. They may want Congress to favor rights for certain people or activities. They may seek cuts in taxes for industry. They may wish Congress to enact or eliminate regulations on business. They may seek changes in the criminal code. They may want to have a piece of forest made into a national park. They may wish to have a certain animal or plant protected by law. Lobbies may try to have someone honored officially with a monument or some other distinction. Lobbyists work on behalf of children, the elderly, teachers, doctors, farmers, businesses, labor unions, and just about any other group you can think of. Name a major special interest in America, and there probably is a lobby for it.

Lobbyists work in many different ways. They may meet personally with members of Congress. They may organize letter-writing campaigns to support passage of new laws. They may call voters and ask them to write to Congress in favor of certain legislation. Lobbyists may put advertisements and articles in newspapers to support their causes. Advertising on television and radio is part of lobbying, too.

❶ *Money talks* means that money has great influence on human behavior.

In lobbying, "money talks❶," as the saying goes. Wealthy groups have an advantage over groups with less money because lobbying is expensive. It requires lots of money to influence the making of laws. So, big groups with big budgets tend to have more influence than small groups with less money. In other words, the rich and powerful can become still more so through lobbying, whereas the poor have no voice at all, or at best a very weak one.

Is this fair? That depends on whom you ask. Big and wealthy groups say they have a right to lobbying. They have a point. In principle, Congress exists to serve all Americans, however rich or poor they may be. It would be unfair to say that businessmen, for example, could not hire lobbyists to represent them.

In practice, however, money – or rather, the lack of it – puts many less powerful groups at a great disadvantage. Even if they have worthy goals, who will listen to them if they lack the money to hire lobbyists who will present their case to lawmakers?

The role of lobbies illustrates a centuries-old struggle in the nation's capital. This struggle puts the poor against the rich, the powerful against the powerless, and the well-organized against the non-organized. In this struggle, "fairness" is often a minor **consideration** – if it is considered at all.

concern, to be thought about.

📰 **WORDS FOR POLITICAL SCIENCE**

✓ disadvantage
✓ enact
✓ lack
✓ legislation
✓ lobby
✓ persuade
✓ require

(convince)

Q u e s t i o n s

01   In your own words, explain what a lobby is.

02   How do lobbies give the rich an advantage over the poor in government?

03   Look at the word **consideration** in the text. What do you think **consideration** means in this context?

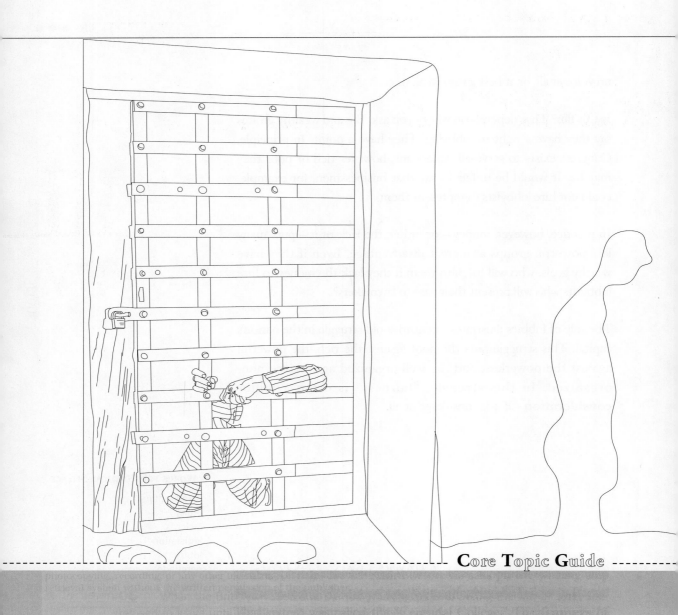

SOCIALSCIENCES III

Psychology

3.1 Ancient Times-the 21st Century: **What Folk Heroes Tell Us**

Paul Bunyan and his ox Babe are famous American folk heroes.

❶ *In turn* means in the same way.

❷ In folklore, a *trickster* is a very clever character.

Even before Europeans came to North America, Native Americans told stories about their folk heroes. Stories about those heroes, in turn❶, told much about the Native Americans.

in the same way.

There was the trickster❷ Rabbit, who was both brave and clever. But Rabbit could not always see the outcome of his own cleverness. In one story, Rabbit caught the sun in a trap!

Folk: very clever character

Early in the mornings, someone was scaring away the wild animals that Rabbit tried to catch. "I will set a trap for him," Rabbit thought. "Then he will not scare away the game any more!"

Rabbit set his trap. It worked. But he had caught the sun! Frightened, Rabbit freed the sun, which rose back into the sky.

This story tells us that Native Americans lived by hunting and trapping, respected cleverness, and knew that even a clever plan did not always get the results one wished!

Another Native American folk hero was Chácopee, the "giant killer." (He had a **counterpart** in European folklore: "Jack the giant killer.")

According to one story, Chácopee destroyed a band of six giants who had killed all the rest of his family. Chácopee killed five of the giants promptly, but the sixth giant was hard to catch and kill. Chácopee finally defeated him by using the giant's own tricks against him. This story shows how Native Americans perceived an important lesson: people will treat you the same way you treat them!

European-Americans had their own folk heroes. Perhaps the most famous was Paul Bunyan, the giant logger. In a way, he stood for America. He was big, strong, honest, and hard-working – the way

Americans liked to see their country.

Paul Bunyan's companion was a giant blue ox named Babe. Together, they had amazing adventures all over the western frontier. In one story, Paul Bunyan dug Lake Michigan so that his giant ox could have a place to drink! This story shows how Americans respect things that are done on a big scale!

One African-American folk hero was John Henry. He was a "steel driver," who dug tunnels through rock for railroads. One day, John Henry had a race with a steam drill. He and the steam drill started digging through rock. Who could dig farther and faster?

John Henry won the race. He dug farther than the steam drill did. But that was the last thing John Henry did. While people around him cheered, he fell down and died. A blood vessel had burst in his brain.

What does this story tell us? Perhaps it is one way to say that even if you are big and strong, some work is better left to machines!

◁⫶) **Chácopee** [tʃákoupiː]

📑 **WORDS FOR PSYCHOLOGY**

✓ counterpart
✓ defeat
✓ destroy
✓ folklore
✓ outcome
✓ respect

Psychology

Questions

01 What is the main point of this passage? Summarize it in one sentence.

02 How does Paul Bunyan reflect American thinking?

03 Look at the word **counterpart** in the passage. What do you think **counterpart** means in this context?

3.2 The 18th-21st century: National Villains

Americans see Benedict Arnold as a villain... but was he?

❶ *Uncle Tom's Cabin*, by Harriet Beecher Stowe, is one of the most important anti-slavery novels in American history.

❷ West Point is now the site of the U.S. Army Academy, which trains officers for the Army.

America has had many heroes, but it also has had many villains. This is easy to understand. It is not enough just to have heroes. One also needs villains to show how strong, brave, and virtuous the heroes are. How can one have a hero without a villain for him to fight and defeat? That is why villains are just as important as heroes are – even if the villains always lose in stories!

Some of America's national villains have been imaginary, like the cruel slave-owner Simon Legree in the novel *Uncle Tom's Cabin*❶. But some American villains were real people. Possibly the greatest of these real-life villains in U.S. history was a soldier named Benedict Arnold. Whether he really was a villain or not, of course, depends on your point of view. Here is his story. See what you think.

Benedict Arnold fought for both sides – American and British – in the war for independence. He started out on the American side. His bravery, courage, and success in battle became famous. He was promoted to the rank of major general.

Yet, soon after that, he was caught planning to hand over the American fort at West Point❷ to the British in return for a large amount of money. Before he could be arrested, Arnold fled to the British side.

Arnold spent the rest of the war fighting for Britain against the Americans as a general. He destroyed part of New London, Connecticut (an important port for American ships) and raided Richmond, Virginia, stealing and destroying supplies the American army needed. In America, his name came to mean a traitor.

Was he really a traitor? From the American viewpoint, he was. He betrayed the Americans. They had the evidence of his treason. حيانة

From the British viewpoint, however, Arnold was loyal to King George III. After all, the Americans were Britain's enemy in a war. What is more, as he fled, Arnold wrote to General George Washington, commander of the American forces, to say that he (Arnold) had acted from love of his country!

What really made Arnold change sides? He needed money. He had many debts and needed some way to pay them. Moreover, Arnold thought the Americans had not really appreciated his service to them.

Why was Arnold so hated? Certainly, he was not **unique**. Many other American officers felt as Arnold did. They felt betrayed by their country after the war, when Congress would not give them pensions for their service. During the war, many American soldiers changed their minds and went to fight for the British. What made Arnold's behavior worse than theirs? Was it just that he wanted money?

Arnold remains a controversial figure. But to this day, in the United States, a traitor is known as a "Benedict Arnold."

🔊 Simon Legree [sáimən ləgríː]

📖 **WORDS FOR PSYCHOLOGY**

✓ appreciate
✓ arrest
✓ betray — حيانت كردن
✓ bravery
✓ courage
✓ evidence
✓ treason
✓ unique
✓ viewpoint
✓ villain

Psychology

Questions

01 According the passage, why is it necessary for every society to have villains?

02 Look at the word **unique** in the passage. What do you think **unique** means in this context?

03 Consider the introductory paragraph to this passage. What does it seem to suggest about the American hatred of Benedict Arnold?

3.3 The 19th Century: The Lincoln Cult

Abraham Lincoln has almost legendary status in America.

Americans show great respect for President Abraham Lincoln, who was killed in 1865, after four years of the War Between the States. Lincoln led the North in that war and was shot and killed by a man who sympathized with the South.

Now, Lincoln's portrait can be seen on the one-cent coin and the five-dollar bill. The Lincoln Memorial, with its great statue of a seated Lincoln, is one of the most famous sights in the nation's capital. Lincoln's name appears on everything from maps to toys[1]. His thin, bearded face – carved on Mount Rushmore[2] – is familiar to everyone, and his words are quoted often.

The "Gettysburg address," the speech Lincoln delivered at Gettysburg[3], Pennsylvania, during the war, is perhaps the most famous speech in U.S. history. Lincoln's birthday was celebrated as a national holiday for many years. He is widely considered the equal of George Washington, first president of the U.S. The name "Lincoln" is often used to describe a man who is very solemn and honest.

In some ways, however, Lincoln's reputation is hard to explain. He was not so respected during his life. What made him such a hero after his death?

Was Lincoln respected, after his death, largely because he was killed while in office? This is not a complete explanation. Other presidents, such as William McKinley, have been killed while in office but have not achieved fame like Lincoln's after they died[4]. Had Lincoln lived longer and died of old age, he might be remembered today as just an average president – competent, but not the equal of George Washington.

Was Lincoln respected after death because of his success? He rose

❶ Lincoln Logs, a famous toy in America, allows children to build the famous log cabin that Lincoln grew up in.

❷ Mount Rushmore is a famous mountain in the U.S. with the faces of four great American presidents, George Washington, Thomas Jefferson, Abraham Lincoln, and Theodore Roosevelt, carved on it.

❸ The battle of Gettysburg was one of the most important battles of the Civil War.

❹ One important difference may be that Lincoln was the first American president to be assassinated.

from **obscure** origins on the western frontier to become president of the United States. That was a great achievement. Yet other presidents such as Andrew Jackson have done the same without becoming as famous as Lincoln.

One explanation for Lincoln's after-death fame is that he died at a special moment in U.S. history, when the country needed a symbol like the one Lincoln provided. In 1865, when Lincoln died, the U.S. had been through four years of civil war. Much of the country had been destroyed. Hundreds of thousands of people were killed. The U.S. literally had been torn apart. The war divided families and created hatreds that still exist more than 100 years later.

At such a time, Americans needed a figure like the dead Lincoln, whom they could revere and use as a symbol of unity and healing. In death, Lincoln served that purpose much better than he could have done in life. His tragic murder made him a hero of sorts, and at last the center of a cult.

🔊 Mount Rushmore
[maunt rʌʃmɔːr]
🔊 William McKinley
[wiljəm məkinli]

Psychology

📑 **WORDS FOR PSYCHOLOGY**

✓ achievement
✓ cult
✓ describe
✓ destroy
✓ hatred
✓ obscure
✓ reputation
✓ respect
✓ revere
✓ sympathize

Questions

01   According to the passage, in what way is the legend of Lincoln historically inaccurate?

02   Look at the word **obscure** in the passage. What do you think **obscure** means in this context?

03   What possible explanation does the author give for Lincoln's popularity after his death?

3.4 The 19th-21st Century: The Elusive "American Character"

Although one often hears people talk about the "American character," there are many different opinions on what the American character is. How can one define it? Does one particular set of beliefs and behaviors unify all, or almost all, Americans?

If such a set of characteristics exists, then it is hard to identify because the U.S. is such a large and diverse nation. Almost anything one says about the United States and its people is likely to be true, and the opposite is likely to be true as well.

❶ Ethnic groups are united by race, language, culture, or national origin.

❷ *Hispanic-Americans* are people from one of the Spanish-speaking American countries like Mexico.

❸ A *soap opera* is a television drama broadcast in the afternoon. Soap operas got that name because they once were sponsored by soap companies.

To illustrate, look at America's ethnic groups❶. What do California's Hispanic-Americans❷ have in common with the German-Americans of Wisconsin? Look at America's cities. What does lofty New York have in common with sprawling Los Angeles?

In every case, the answer is: practically nothing. Moreover, when one does find some shared behavior or belief among all (or nearly all) Americans, it is probably something that seems trivial, such as admiration for a certain popular singer or the habit of watching a particular soap opera❸ on television. Indeed, it has been said that television is about the only thing that brings all Americans together.

That remark about television, perhaps, brings us close to an understanding of the American character at the start of the 21st century.

Today, we see an America that has changed dramatically over the past 100 years. It is located on the same continent as the America of 1900, and still has the same flag and unit of currency; but otherwise, these two Americas are almost as different as imperial China and imperial Rome.

The very process of thinking has changed dramatically. We now have given over much of our thinking to machines. Computers with

"artificial intelligence" make many decisions for us. They decide everything from when we will get medical care to when and how far we may move our cars in traffic.

What is more, Americans accept this situation. They have learned to expect that machines will control their lives in countless ways. Machines will determine how people spend their money, what they will buy at a market, and how they will spend their leisure time. To a certain extent, even their tastes and opinions are machine-made, so that Americans take their programming, in a sense, from machines. Not many years ago, humans were programmers, and machines took programming from them. Now, that relationship is being reversed.

eg) Napoleon threatened to starve the country into submission.
> = Surrender

In this context, think back to that earlier remark about television. It unites Americans because it supplies much of their programming. They believe what television tells them to believe, and they do what television tells them to do. So, one might say that to be American today is, in part, to take orders from machines.

That condition would have seemed unbelievable to most Americans at the start of the 20th century. As the 21st century opens, however, rule by machines is accepted as a fact of life.

Submission FIND new

Is this slavery? Perhaps it is. And is this **subservience** to technology the characteristic that defines Americans nowadays? That is a sobering view, but much evidence supports it.

📑 **WORDS FOR PSYCHOLOGY**

✓ character
✓ characteristic
✓ define
✓ determine
✓ diverse
✓ identify
✓ lofty
✓ opinion
✓ slavery
✓ unify

Psychology

always obeying another person and doing everything they want you to do.

Questions

eg. Don remained entirely subservient to his Father.

01 What point about the American character does the author make here? Summarize this passage in one sentence.

02 How does the author think Americans have changed in the last 100 years?

03 What is the author's opinion of these changes? How do you know? Explain.

04 Look at the word **subservience** in the passage. What do you think **subservience** means in this context?

3.5   The 19th-20th Century: Americans and "Aliens"

America claims to be a nation open to immigrants, but that is not always the case.

❶ Here, *aliens* means people from other countries.

❷ A famous poem about the Statue of Liberty reads "Give me your tired, your poor, your huddled masses." This expresses the open attitude towards immigration that America is supposed to have.

❸ *Time and again* means often or repeatedly.

One strange aspect of life in the United States has always been its attitude toward "aliens❶." Americans like to think of themselves as "a nation of immigrants," ready to welcome newcomers. That is at least the message of the Statue of Liberty in New York harbor. The statue was built, in part, as a message of welcome to immigrants. In principle, then, America's door was open❷. Reality, however, has been different. "Aliens" in America often have had to overcome great obstacles and powerful opposition.

Although most Americans are descended from immigrants who came to America much earlier, Americans are suspicious – and often hostile – toward modern immigrants. This is especially true when modern immigrants come from places with very different customs. Recent immigrants from southern Asia, for example, have found many Americans hostile toward them. "Aliens," the newcomers discovered, were not welcome at all.

Time and again❸, this phenomenon has occurred in American history. Immigrants arrived there expecting to find a land filled with opportunity. Instead, the new arrivals got a cold, if not violent, reception. When large numbers of Irish immigrants landed in the U.S. during the 19th century, they were treated as something less than human. One cartoonist for a major American newspaper drew the Irish as apes! Americans thought: let aliens remain aliens, and let would-be immigrants stay abroad, where they belonged!

This opposition actually was more noise than anything else. In practice, the immigrants usually were allowed to stay. Kellys lived next to Schmidts, and Fischettis had Campbells for neighbors. In time, the immigrants, or at least their children, were accepted as genuine Americans.

Still, anti-alien feeling grew strong enough to influence U.S. politics at times. A case in point⁰ is the brief career of the American Party, also known as the "Know-nothings," in the 1850s. Many Americans of Protestant descent (the most powerful religious and ethnic group in the U.S. at that time) became frightened when numerous Irish and German immigrants, who were mostly Roman Catholics, came over from Europe. The Protestants found their dominance was challenged. Suddenly, theirs was no longer entirely a white, Protestant, English-speaking society. "Aliens" had gotten in.

In response, some Americans formed a secret anti-immigrant society. They promised to oppose Roman Catholicism, discriminate against the immigrants, and, in elections, vote only for Protestants born in the U.S. If anyone asked about their group's beliefs and activities, they were supposed to say, "I know nothing!" So, they became known as the Know-nothings.

Opposition to the immigrants was so strong for a while that the "Know-nothings" became very powerful in America. They organized as a political party, the American Party, in 1854. The new movement disturbed Abraham Lincoln. He pointed out that the United States was founded on the idea that "all men are created equal," and no exceptions should be made.

The American Party, however, lasted only a short time. The immigrants soon were accepted, or at least tolerated. Why? Perhaps it was because Americans often prefer to follow "the path of least resistance." It was easier to admit the immigrants than to fight them. Before long, the "aliens" had ceased to be aliens at all!

❹ *A case in point* means an example.

◁ Campbells [kǽmbəlz]
◁ Fischettis [fiʃétiːz]
◁ Schmidts [ʃmits]

Psychology

📑 **WORDS FOR PSYCHOLOGY**
✓ attitude
✓ descend
✓ discriminate
✓ dominance
✓ genuine
✓ hostile
✓ immigrant
✓ numerous
✓ obstacle
✓ overcome

Questions

01 What point does the author make about anti-immigrant feelings in America?

02 The author says in paragraph 4, "Kellys lived next to Schmidts, and Fischettis had Campbells for neighbors." Why does the author mention these names? What do they represent here? Explain.

3.6 The 19th-20th Century: The Importance of Uncle Sam

America has many national symbols, but none is better known and more versatile than Uncle Sam, the tall, thin, bearded man dressed in the colors of the U.S. flag.

I WANT YOU
FOR U.S. ARMY
NEAREST RECRUITING STATION

Uncle Sam is a familiar image. He appears here on a famous recruiting poster.

Uncle Sam is used to represent the American government, the federal government in particular, or the nation as a whole. His lean features can be made to look friendly or hostile, sad or happy, proud or shocked, and his tall stature makes him a good symbol of U.S. dominance in many fields. He even has the same initials as the United States – "U.S."

Uncle Sam often appears as a character in fiction and is portrayed on television with gentle humor. Moreover, Uncle Sam's image has great "brand recognition," as advertisers would say. Almost everyone in the world recognizes Uncle Sam. His image is as familiar as that of Don Quixote or Santa Claus. And since the character is free of **copyright**, any artist or writer is free to use Uncle Sam.

Perhaps the most famous image of Uncle Sam was painted by American artist James Montgomery Flagg for an Army recruiting poster in World War I. In the picture, a solemn Uncle Sam looks directly at the viewer. The caption reads, "I want you for U.S. Army." Almost a century later, the poster is still famous.

❶ Here, *around* means in existence.

But Uncle Sam was not invented for that Army poster. Uncle Sam, or at least his name as a symbol of the U.S. government, already had been around❶ for more than 100 years before Flagg painted Uncle Sam's picture. The earliest known reference to "Uncle Sam" was in an American newspaper in 1813. Apparently, the name was already widely used in that context then.

The well-known image of Uncle Sam is thought to have been taken from a food inspector named Samuel Wilson, who examined barrels of beef supplied to the U.S. Army in the 19th century. The barrels were marked "U.S." As a joke, someone said the initials referred to "Uncle Sam" Wilson. According to this story, Wilson looked much like the Uncle Sam we know today, and that remark about "Uncle Sam" is how the character originated.

Is the story true? We do not know. Whether or not Uncle Sam was based on a real person, however, this much is certain. The whole world knows him now!

◁) Don Quixote [dɑn kihóuti]
◁) James Montgomery Flagg
[dʒeimz mɑntgʌ́məri flæg]

📑 WORDS FOR PSYCHOLOGY

✓ originate
✓ portray
✓ recognize
✓ represent
✓ stature
✓ versatile

Psychology

Questions

01   Why is Uncle Sam familiar all over the world? This passage gives several reasons. Explain them in your own words.

02   Why does the author mention Don Quixote and Santa Claus in this passage? Explain.

03   Look at the word **copyright** in the passage. What do you think **copyright** means in this context?

04   What theory does the author give for the possible origin of Uncle Sam?

3.7 The 19th-20th Century: The Need for a Frontier

When Americans hear the word "frontier," they think of new worlds to be explored or new challenges to be faced and overcome. When 19th-century American historian Frederick Jackson Turner looked at his nation and its thinking, he decided that America was a frontier-centered society, and the individual American was basically a frontier person.

Turner thought this attitude explained many things about American history and thought. He traced many characteristics of Americans back to their long experience with the frontier. Americans were always "moving on." Through much of their history, they had moved on literally, toward the new lands of the western frontier.

Turner's view about the frontier's importance to Americans had a strong influence. It helped to explain why Americans have always looked toward a frontier. In fact, they needed a frontier. As a nation and a society, America was hard to imagine without a frontier. But what were they supposed to do when the geographical frontier vanished around the year 1900?

When the geographical frontier disappeared at last, in the early 20th century❶, American popular culture responded in two ways.

The first response was nostalgia, with a strong element of escapism. People still longed for a frontier that could provide escape from the pressures of modern living. To satisfy that longing, radio, movies, and television depicted an American West that never was: a modern version of 19th-century dime novels❷ about a free, exciting life on the western frontier. TV shows such as *The Lone Ranger, Bonanza* and *The Rifleman* regaled viewers with dramas about the European-American conquest of the western lands.

In these works, the "old West" was romanticized to the point of absurdity. The actual cowboys, marshals, and outlaws of the 1800s

❶ With the purchase of Alaska in 1868, there was no longer any place in North America where the United States could expand.

❷ *Dime novels* were cheap novels with a highly romanticized view of life on the western frontier.

might never have recognized themselves as portrayed on screen, had they been[3] able to watch the TV shows and movies made about them in the 20th century. But a realistic picture of the "old West" was the last thing 20th-century audiences wanted. Instead, they sought fantasy and escapism, which the entertainment industry was happy to provide.

[3] had they been ... = if they had been ...

an essential part of sth

For much of the 20th century, then, "the western" was a **mainstay** of American entertainment, and shows about frontier days had a huge and eager audience. But at last, entertainment exhausted even the abundant lore of the American West. The audience for westerns diminished in the 1970s and 1980s.

Yet the need for a frontier remained. So, America's second response to that need was to create new frontiers in the imagination. It was no accident that President John F. Kennedy's administration in the early 1960s defined its agenda as "the New Frontier." That was what the country craved.

The fresh frontiers of which Americans dreamed, however, were unlike the old western frontier. The old frontier was geographical. The new frontiers were social, intellectual, and even cosmic in scope. Here, "cosmic" is no exaggeration. When Kennedy started the U.S. program to put astronauts on the moon, the American frontier suddenly shifted from the old West to outer space. The outcome of this shift would transform American entertainment yet again – and shape the dreams and hopes of several generations of Americans then unborn.

📄 **WORDS FOR PSYCHOLOGY**

- ✓ abundant
- ✓ depict
- ✓ exhaust
- ✓ explore
- ✓ frontier
- ✓ mainstay
- ✓ regale
- ✓ romanticize
- ✓ trace
- ✓ transform
- ✓ vanish

Psychology

Questions

01   According to the passage, how has the concept of a frontier influenced American thinking?

02   Look at the word **mainstay** in the passage. What do you think **mainstay** means in this context?

03   According to the passage, how did Americans respond when they finally completed the western expansion?

3.8 The 20th Century: "Star Trek" and American Thinking

Captain Kirk was a typically American character, essentially a cowboy in space.

The original *Star Trek* television series of the 1960s, about a starship exploring the galaxy, was unmistakably an American show. A Russian or Italian or German would not have produced a show like *Star Trek* because it was rooted deeply in American ideas, traditions, and institutions.

Star Trek was science fiction, and for much of the 20th century, science fiction was mainly an American art form. Space travel in particular was a specialty of American science fiction writers. So, *Star Trek* stood for a tradition in American popular literature.

The show also was based on a concept that had been used successfully in many other American TV series: travelers exploring a frontier. American TV shows such as the western drama *Wagon Train* had made good use of a frontier setting for adventure stories. Now, the time was ideal to transfer the frontier from America's western frontier (which had vanished years before) to outer space, which Americans were only starting to explore.

That transition was easy to make. Only a few years before *Star Trek* appeared on television, then President Kennedy had announced his "New Frontier" programs and committed the U.S. to putting astronauts on the moon. So, the time was right for *Star Trek*.

Other parallels between *Star Trek* and the U.S. during the 1960s were easy to see. America's foreign rivals at that time – primarily the Soviets and the Chinese – had their counterparts on *Star Trek*, in the Klingons and Romulans. Just as China and the Soviet Union were non-democratic societies, so the Romulan and Klingon empires were **authoritarian** in character.

Then there was *Star Trek*'s typically American attitude toward technology. When applied correctly, it was a good servant. When applied wrongly, however, it could become a terrible master. Many *Star Trek* episodes showed what happened when technology "went wrong." The message of *Star Trek* was something like this. You can trust technology. Just keep it under tight control!

The practical side of the American character was essential to *Star Trek* stories, too. Captain Kirk had responsibilities. He was the "man on the spot❶," to use a classic American expression. He had to make tough decisions. Viewers were forced, again and again, to address the question: "In this situation, what would one do?" Answers to that question supplied the basis for *Star Trek* stories and gave the show a loyal audience for decades.

❶ *Man on the spot* refers to someone, usually a leader, who is in a difficult situation and must quickly think of a solution.

🔊 **Klingons** [klíɲɑnz]
🔊 **Romulans** [róumjulənz]

Though the original *Star Trek* series was set in the far future, it really was about America in the 1960s. A few years after *Star Trek* appeared, the United States and the rest of the world would change dramatically – and so would the other TV series and movies based on it. One might view the whole *Star Trek* phenomenon as a record of a rapidly changing America and its shifting place in the world.

📋 **WORDS FOR PSYCHOLOGY**

✓ apply
✓ commit
✓ counterpart
✓ essential
✓ explore
✓ tradition
✓ transfer
✓ transition

Psychology

Questions

01 What connections does the author make between *Star Trek* and the history of America?

02 In your own words, explain some of the ways in which *Star Trek* reflected the American character.

03 What made Captain Kirk a popular character in America?

04 Look at the word **authoritarian** in the passage. What do you think **authoritarian** means in this context?

3.9 The 20th Century: Shaping Public Opinion

Family Feud was a popular game show in which families tried to guess the results of opinion polls.

When statistical methods are used to sample and report public opinion, the result is an "opinion poll." In the second half of the 20th century, gauging public opinion became a big business. Almost everyone, it seemed, wanted to know what the public was thinking.

Companies wanted to increase their profits. So, they used opinion surveys to find out what people wanted to buy. Politicians wanted to get votes. So, they used opinion surveys to find out what voters were thinking. Interest groups wanted to promote their social agendas. So, they used opinion **polls** to find out what public image they had.

In short, nearly anyone who made important decisions consulted an opinion survey at one time or another. That was why opinion surveys became an everyday part of American life. "Survey says ..." became one of the most familiar expressions in the country.

Thanks to statistical analysis aided by computers, it became possible to predict, in many cases, how the public as a whole would respond to something, such as a political platform❶, a new product, or a candidate for elected office. This knowledge helped greatly in planning everything from consumer goods to election campaigns.

These methods for sampling opinion, however, could affect public opinion as well as reflect it. In other words, a public opinion survey could both measure and change public opinion. The result was a whole industry meant to shape and redirect, rather than merely report, people's views.

How did this new industry operate? It had many devices. The

❶ A *political platform* is a summary of what a political party promises to do if elected.

"selected quote" was one of them.

"Selected" quotes from individuals on some issue could be presented as representative quotes from the public. But there was a great difference. If all the selected quotes were selected because they favored or opposed something, then the quotes were not representative; that is, they did not tell what the public really thought.

Also, questions could be worded in a misleading way. Through clever choice of words in an opinion survey, the survey taker could make it look as if the public favored or opposed something that really was not an issue at all.

These and other tricks helped make the opinion survey into a tool for reshaping and redirecting public opinion. When the misleading "results" of such a survey were published, they had some influence on actual public opinion. "If this is what most people think," a reader might say to himself after reading the unreliable results, "then maybe it is true!"

The effect of any single "survey" might be small. Yet this effect, repeated time and again over several months, might actually sway public opinion to a great extent. The process was like wind acting on a ship. Wind might push a ship only slightly off course; but the outcome, after many hours, was to move the ship far away.

📑 **WORDS FOR PSYCHOLOGY**

✓ affect
✓ analysis
✓ gauge
✓ opinion
✓ predict
✓ promote
✓ reflect

Psychology

Questions

01 In your own words, explain what a public opinion survey is and how it works.

02 Look at the word **polls** in the passage. What do you think **polls** means in this context?

03 In your own words, explain how and why people seek to manipulate the results of opinion surveys.

04 Why does the author mention a ship in the final paragraph? What is the ship supposed to stand for? Explain.

3.10 The 20th Century: How To Sell Anything

The Coco-Cola company is famous for its highly effective advertising.

❶ This comes from a popular American saying, "He could sell refrigerators in Alaska." The saying is used to describe a person who is very persuasive.

In the early 20th century, President Calvin Coolidge was quoted as saying, "The business of America is business." Whether or not he actually said it is not important. In either case, it shows what kind of society America had for much of its history. It was a mercantile society, in which merchants played an important role and could become very rich and powerful.

A merchant sells things. Selling requires advertising. That is why it might be more accurate to say instead, "The business of America is advertising." Because they wanted to sell almost anything one could imagine, from cotton to coal, Americans became experts at advertising. At their best, U.S. advertisers could "sell refrigerators in Alaska❶," one might say. They could sell almost anything to nearly anyone, and they did so, over much of the world.

Name a product – aircraft, aspirin, automobiles, flour, floor tile, medicines, motors, wire, washing machines, or whatever else – and America advertised it around the world. And even when the thing being sold was an idea or principle instead of a commercial product, advertising was both important and carefully **crafted**.

It had to be carefully crafted because the advertiser had only a brief opportunity to interest a buyer. Someone might see or hear an advertisement for only a couple of seconds. In that short time, the advertiser had to put a product or message into the person's thoughts, so that he or she would remember it favorably when the time came to buy something.

Moreover, the message had to be specific. It was not enough just to say, "Drink soda." The message had to be: "Drink our soda!" And it had to be presented in a memorable and pleasing way.

That was a challenge. But to meet it, advertisers had three mighty tools: words, music, and images. They used all three to good effect.

Words often took the form of slogans. Some slogans used during World War II, for example, are still quoted. When people want to emphasize the need for secrecy and security, they say, "Loose lips sink ships❷!" The old wartime slogan still works because it expressed an important principle (careless talk is dangerous) in a rhyme with only four short words.

Music helped, too. A slogan set to music is easier to remember than a slogan alone. But perhaps the most important part of advertising was the image. As the saying goes, a picture really is worth 1,000 words. So, America advertisers brought about a whole new era in advertising art. They had the help of brilliant illustrators, from Maxfield Parrish to Andy Warhol.

Among the most famous images in advertising was for a soft drink company. Every year, the company would release posters that showed Santa Claus with the company's drink. For these pictures, artist Haddon Sundblom drew Santa Claus in a bright red suit trimmed in white. The pictures were so appealing that they not only sold the drink, but also helped create the modern image of Santa Claus. Some people actually thought the company had invented Santa Claus to sell its drinks!

❷ *Loose lips sink ships* meant that careless talk might give the enemy vital information.

🔊 Andy Warhol [ǽndi wɔ́ːrhɔːl]
🔊 Calvin Coolidge [kǽlvin kúːlidʒ]
🔊 Haddon Sundblom [hǽdən súndblɑm]
🔊 Maxfield Parrish [mǽksfiːld pǽriʃ]

📑 **WORDS FOR PSYCHOLOGY**

✓ accurate
✓ appealing
✓ brilliant
✓ release
✓ require
✓ specific

Psychology

Questions

01   Why is advertising so important in America?

02   What are the three tools which advertisers use?

03   Based on the information in the passage, can you infer what characteristics an effective slogan should have?

04   Look at the word **crafted** in the passage. What do you think **crafted** means in this context?

3.11 The 20th Century: The UFO Phenomenon

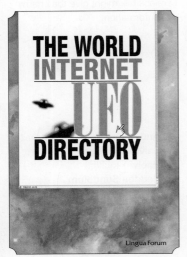

The UFO phenomenon is big news on the Internet, as this book shows.

❶ A *boomerang* is an Australian hunting tool shaped like a shallow " ∨ " and thrown through the air.

In the second half of the 1900s, an odd new idea became popular in the United States. People began to think that "space people," or intelligent beings from other planets, were visiting Earth in spaceships shaped like saucers. Suddenly, talk of "flying saucers" and "spacemen" was everywhere, and many Americans came to believe that visitors from other worlds were zipping through Earth's skies. Thus began a strange transformation of popular thinking that changed America profoundly by the end of the century.

The "flying saucer" era began in 1947, when a pilot flying near Mount Rainier in Washington state reported seeing unusual, silvery craft in the air nearby. He said they moved like saucers skipped across a pond. The press called the objects "flying saucers," though the pilot did not say the objects were saucer-shaped. (He thought they were shaped more like boomerangs❶.)

Flying saucers captured the imagination of the American public. Hollywood was especially interested. Here was a whole new set of fantastic stories waiting to be told! Movies about flying saucers began showing in theaters. Some were cheap and crude. Others were spectacular and well-made, such as the famous 1955 movie *This Island Earth*, in which fictional aliens visit Earth in search of fresh energy supplies.

In that movie, the aliens were friendly. In other movies, including *Earth versus the Flying Saucers* (1956), the aliens were hostile. *Earth versus the Flying Saucers* showed flying saucers attacking Earth. Scenes from both movies are still impressive, half a century after they were made.

Why was America fascinated with flying saucers in the late 1940s and 1950s? The country was tired and nervous then. World War II had just ended. People wanted peace and quiet. Instead, they heard stories about ships from other planets – possibly enemy planets –

visiting Earth. Was another war, this time between planets rather than nations, about to start? Were the spacemen friends or **foes**, or just imaginary? Questions like these had Americans looking at the skies and wondering what was happening.

The flying saucer phenomenon changed over the years. The saucers became known as "unidentified flying objects," or UFOs. The difference of opinion about the "space people," however, did not go away. Some people thought the aliens, if they existed, were friendly. Others thought the aliens must be hostile.

The "friendly alien" image was the basis for another famous picture about UFOs in 1977, 30 years after the first "flying saucer" case. Steven Spielberg's movie *Close Encounters of the Third Kind* showed a peaceful meeting between aliens and humans in the western desert of the United States. In the movie, the aliens communicate with humans by music. Later, Spielberg had another success with his movie *E.T.* (1982), about a friendly alien stranded on Earth. Both movies contributed to Americans' interest in UFOs and the beings that were thought to ride in them.

The question, however, remained: were there really any aliens "out there❷" at all? Were friendly (or unfriendly) "space people" actually visiting Earth, or was the whole UFO phenomenon a fantasy? As the year 2000 approached, there were still arguments on both sides.

It was amazing to see how the UFO phenomenon had changed Americans' outlook on their world, their universe, and themselves in less than a single human lifetime.

❷ In this context, *out there* means in outer space or on other planets.

🔊 Mount Rainier [maunt rəníər]

Psychology

📖 **WORDS FOR PSYCHOLOGY**

✓ approach
✓ argument
✓ capture
✓ contribute
✓ crude
✓ hostile
✓ outlook
✓ strand
✓ transformation

Questions

01 How did American fears and apprehensions after World War II contribute to interest in flying saucers?

02 Look at the word **foes** in the passage. What do you think **foes** means in this context?

03 In what way did Hollywood present opposing views regarding flying saucers?

3.12 The 20th Century: "Environmental Awareness"

Environmentally friendly products are now big business.

Americans have always had two different views about the environment. On the one hand, they thought forests, lakes, and other resources were there to be used for something. Forests should be cut to build houses. Lakes and rivers should be fished. Mountains should be mined for rock. This attitude is called "exploitation." It means that the environment exists for people to use and consume.

For many years, this view **prevailed** [*dominant*] in the United States. The country was so big that there seemed no end to its resources. So, Americans cut down forests, killed whole species of animals, and polluted water almost everywhere. Huge amounts of trash – the output of the American "consumer economy" – piled up. Indeed, the biggest human-made object on Earth was a trash dump in New York state!

In the late 20th century, however, that attitude started to change. Americans started to see that environmental resources were not unlimited, after all. Resources like clean air and clean water were running out. Many species were disappearing. People were polluting the land and water in ways that would take a long time to clean up, if they could be cleaned up at all. Seeing this, Americans responded with a change in thinking.

❶ The Environmental Protection Agency, or EPA, monitors businesses to make sure that they are not damaging the environment.

Around 1970, "environmental awareness" became important to Americans. The U.S. passed laws to protect the environment. The U.S. government even started the Environmental Protection Agency❶ to save disappearing species and control pollution.

In stores, "environment-friendly" products became popular. People thought that buying "environment-friendly" products – that is, products with few or no harmful effects on the environment –

would help to protect the environment for future generations.

Along the way, however, "environmental awareness" became a product itself. It was a commodity, something to be packaged and sold, like soap or bread. Whole businesses grew up to market environmental awareness. It became fashionable. Therefore, it went on sale. To show one's environmental awareness, one could buy a bumper sticker for one's car, a button with a message to wear on one's coat, or a magazine that showed your interest in the environment.

As environmental awareness became a commodity and went on sale, it also developed its own set of images for use in advertising, such as colorful birds and flowers, friendly whales, and so forth. A whole industry of "environmentally aware" advertising developed to sell products.

Perhaps it helped to protect the environment. Maybe environmental awareness prevented the marketing of some harmful products. But in the end, the original goal of "environmental awareness" changed. That awareness, at first, showed respect and concern for the environment. Soon, however, environmental awareness became part of the "consumer economy" that had created that giant trash dump in New York! Environmental awareness had become something entirely different from what was originally intended.

WORDS FOR PSYCHOLOGY

✓ attitude
✓ awareness
✓ commodity
✓ consume
✓ disappear
✓ prevail
✓ resource

Psychology

Questions

01 What drove the American belief in exploitation? What caused Americans to change their beliefs?

02 What do you think author's attitude is concerning environmental awareness?

03 Look at the word **prevailed** in the passage. What do you think **prevailed** means in this context?

3.13 The 20th Century: Americans and the "Underdog"

Americans often prefer people who are at a disdvantage.

A mericans like to think that they favor the "underdog," the weaker party in a fight. Certain evidence supports this view.

In baseball, America's "national pastime," the "underdog" team is often a favorite. When an underdog team wins, the audience feels pleased, because it shows that the favored team – the one with the better players and reputation – is not sure to win a game. Even a relatively weak team may win by playing well.

Time and again, an underdog team has defeated a favored team. That is what makes baseball interesting. Victory does not always go to the strong and famous. On the contrary, the underdog can win, and sometimes does!

That principle **underlies** much of American popular culture as well. Some of the most famous figures in America entertainment are underdogs who overcome odds that are not in their favor.

❶ In this story, the rabbit tricks his enemy into throwing him into a briar patch – where, in fact, the rabbit lives.

One of America's best-known stories for children is about a rabbit who, though smaller and weaker than the animals that prey on him, escapes them through clever use of his own weakness❶. Native American folklore describes how children – the smallest and weakest of humans – survive and even get rewards through intelligence and bravery. Comic books, animated cartoons, musical comedies, movies, and many other kinds of entertainment have used this theme time and again, with great success.

Why does the underdog's story appeal so strongly to Americans? Perhaps one reason can be found in American history.

The American colonies fought Britain in the war for independence during the late 1700s. Britain was by far the stronger power. The colonies were the "underdog" in this war. Still, Americans won, partly by fighting well and partly with the help of a powerful ally, France.

The British surrender at Yorktown in 1781, at the end of the war, was a classic victory of the underdog over a stronger opponent. This case and others from history have encouraged Americans to see themselves as the underdog in a fight, and to favor anyone else who faces a similar situation in sports or entertainment.

Sports and entertainment, however, are not exactly the real world. Instead, they are special worlds, simplified and artificial, where many factors that work in the real world are ignored or removed. And in the real world, those factors make a happy ending – that is, victory for the underdog – very unlikely. That is not a story that entertainers like to tell, but it is much closer to the reality of history.

Psychology

📑 **WORDS FOR PSYCHOLOGY**

✓ appeal
✓ defeat
✓ encourage
✓ evidence
✓ favor
✓ odds
✓ survive
✓ underlie

Questions

01 Why does the author mention baseball in this passage? Explain in one sentence.

02 Look at the word **underlies** in the passage. What do you think **underlies** means in this context?

03 In your own words, explain the historical roots of America's fascination with underdogs.

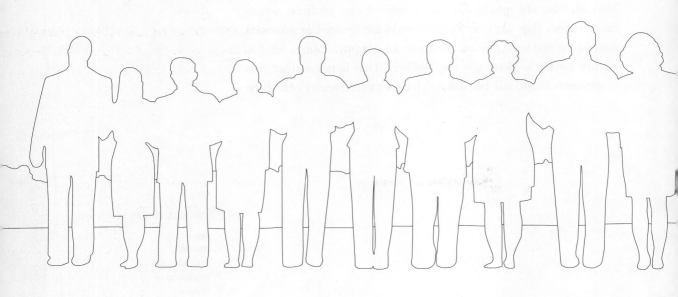

SOCIAL SCIENCES IV

Sociology

4.1 The 18th-20th Century: "Equality" and Reality

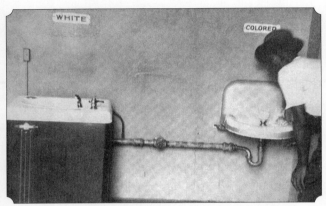
Segregation is just one example of inequality in America's history.

❶ In addition to formally declaring America's independence from Britain, the Declaration of Independence outlines the values and ideals that the United States is supposed to embody.

❷ One of the ways that slavery was justified in America was by claiming that Africans were actually a different, lesser species of human.

❸ The Emancipation Proclamation, signed by President Lincoln in 1863, formally ended slavery in the U.S.

Americans have a long history of confusing ideals with realities. Another way to say this is that Americans often honor an ideal but practice something else entirely in real life. A good example is "equality." As an ideal, it is widely honored. As a way of life, however, it is highly restricted.

America's Declaration of Independence❶ described all people as "created equal." This is true, up to a point. Humans all belong to the same species and live on the same planet. Otherwise, however, inequality – not equality – is the rule. That rule applies in the United States, as everywhere else.

In the 18th century, when the Declaration of Independence was written, America was far from having social equality. There were rich people and poor people. The rich, of course, had more privileges than the poor. There also were masters and slaves. Slaves were actually considered less than human and were treated in the same way❷. They were exploited for labor and even tortured when they did not work well.

Conditions changed in the 19th century. Technically, slavery was abolished in the United States during the war years of the 1860s❸. But was the change more in word than in reality? Were slaves still slaves, even if they were called "workers" or "laborers"? The **distinction** between a laborer and a slave was not always easy to see.

After 1865, it was true that slavery as practiced on southern farms before the War Between the States had been abolished in name. Yet had it been abolished in fact? Did it matter much whether a person worked as a laborer on a southern farm or in a northern factory, if that person was, so to speak, chained to the job in either case❹? The basic inequality – servant versus master – remained, even when the master was called one's "employer" or "boss" and the servant was called an "employee."

Certainly, no one would say that Native Americans enjoyed the same privileges as European-Americans. As the latter moved westward, they simply relocated or killed the Native Americans who stood in their way, and stole their land in the process. Was this the work of a nation that really thought everyone was "created equal"?

❹ In the late 1800s, there were no unions to protect the rights of workers, and conditions in factories were terrible.

WORDS FOR SOCIOLOGY

✓ abolish
✓ equality
✓ exploit
✓ ideal
✓ inequality
✓ privilege
✓ restrict

Sociology

Questions

01   In your own words, describe the main point of this passage.

02   Look at the word **distinction** in the passage. What do you think **distinction** means in this context?

03   In paragraph 5, what point does the author make about the abolition of slavery?

4.2 The 19ᵗʰ Century: The Politics of Corruption

"THAT'S WHAT'S THE MATTER."

Boss Tweed. "As long as I count the Votes, what are you going to do about it? say?"

William M. Tweed was "boss" of New York City.

❶ A *social safety net* is a system or program to prevent people from falling into poverty. An example is the Social Security system in the United States.

I n New York during the 1800s, some people rose to great fame and power, then fell back to a low station in life. That was the story of William M. Tweed (1823-1878). For a while, Tweed was one of the most powerful men in America, but he died in prison, disgraced and a failure.

Tweed was the boss, or leader, of Tammany Hall, a political organization in New York. Although "Boss Tweed" started his career on a humble level, as a furniture maker and fireman, he got elected to public office and, with help from his friends, rose to the top in politics. He became a congressman and a state senator.

Tweed wanted money. New York had plenty of it. So, Tweed and his associates **looted** the city's treasury. How much money they stole in this way is not known. Possibly, the "Tweed ring," as Tweed and his gang were called, stole more than 100 million dollars.

How was Tweed able to do this? His organization was very powerful. It was also popular. Tweed appealed to the many poor immigrants in New York. When immigrants arrived, the Tweed organization helped them find homes and get jobs. Tweed's group gave the immigrants protection and security. (Today, we would call it a "social safety net❶.") In return, the immigrants voted for Tweed's men.

This system worked – for a while. It made Tweed very rich and powerful. But then, one of Tweed's men became dissatisfied. He thought he had received too little money. He gave evidence to a newspaper that the Tweed ring was robbing the city. At first, Tweed did not seem worried. "What are you going to do about it?" he said when asked about his corruption.

But the law caught up with Tweed. He was put on trial and

convicted. He spent a year in jail. His troubles, however, were not over. After he got out of jail, the state of New York sued him for 6 million dollars. Tweed fled from New York to Cuba in 1875, and from there to Spain, but was caught and sent back to New York in 1876. Two years later, he died in prison.

Was Boss Tweed a great criminal, or just typical of his time? Whatever one thinks of him, Tweed showed how high an ordinary person could rise in New York during the 1800s ... and how far one could fall.

🔊 Tammany Hall [tǽməni hɔːl]
🔊 William M. Tweed
    [wíljəm em twiːd]

📑 **WORDS FOR SOCIOLOGY**

✓ convict
✓ corruption
✓ criminal
✓ loot
✓ ordinary
✓ security
✓ typical

Questions

01   How was Tweed able to gain such power in New York politics?

02   The passage says about Boss Tweed: "'What are you going to do about it?' he said when asked about his corruption." What does that quote tell you about Tweed? Explain.

03   Look at the word **looted** in the passage. What do you think **looted** means in this context?

04   What led to Tweed's fall from power?

Sociology

4.3 The 19th-20th Century: **The Irish in America**

Working in coal mines and on railroads, Irish immigrants provided much of America's labor force.

For much of American history, the words "Irish" and "immigrant" were almost **inseparable**. This was because huge numbers of Irish immigrants came to America in the 19th and 20th centuries. Between 1820 and 1978, almost 5 million people from Ireland came to live in the United States. That was almost 10 percent of all immigrants to the U.S. from other countries. In other words, about one in every 10 immigrants to America was Irish!

Why did so many people from Ireland move to America? For one thing, there was more opportunity in America. In the early 19th century, Ireland's biggest industry was farming. There was little opportunity to make money. In the U.S., however, things were different. A worker in America could make much more money than a farmer in Ireland. So, the Irish began moving to America. They helped to build public works such as the great Erie Canal❶.

❶ The Erie Canal was a vast canal system that connected the Great Lakes with the Atlantic Ocean.

Then, in the mid-19th century, the Irish had an even stronger reason to leave Ireland for America. A disease destroyed Ireland's potato crop, starting in 1845. Potatoes were important to the Irish, and people could not get enough to eat. This horrible time was called the "Irish famine." It killed about a million people in all.

Desperate to get out of Ireland, people sailed for the U.S. In 1846, about 92,500 Irish immigrants came to America. That number increased quickly. In 1850, there were more than 200,000 Irish immigrants. Over 10 years, almost two million people came from Ireland to the United States. That was about one-fourth of Ireland's population! In all, between 1820 and 1920, almost 4.5 million Irish immigrants settled in America.

Many Irish immigrants were poor. In the U.S., they worked as laborers. They became coal miners and railroad workers. Between 1861 and 1865, many of the Irish fought in the War Between the States. After the war, the Irish became powerful in American politics because there were so many of them. Big cities like New York, Boston and San Francisco had Irish mayors. Some of the Irish also became very successful in business.

In the U.S. today, one can still see many things the Irish immigrants built. One can also see the Irish influence in America by looking at a telephone book. Note how many names in it are Irish, like Kelly, O'Toole, and O'Brien. Without the Irish, America would have been a very different country!

 Erie Canal [iːri kənǽl]

📑 **WORDS FOR SOCIOLOGY**

✓ desperate
✓ famine
✓ huge
✓ inseparable
✓ settle

Sociology

Questions

01 Look at the word **inseparable** in the passage. What do you think **inseparable** means in this context?

02 In your own words, describe what factors brought the Irish to America.

03 In the final paragraph, why does the author mention several Irish names? Explain in one sentence.

4.4 The 19th-20th Century: The Japanese-American Experience

❶ *To say the least* means undoubtedly or without question.

The experience of Japanese-Americans has been varied, to say the least**❶**. It has ranged from success in business, science, the arts, and politics to official persecution during World War II, when more than 100,000 Japanese-Americans were arrested and made prisoners in their own country.

Japanese immigration to the U.S. and its territories began in 1868, when 153 Japanese migrants sailed from Yokohama to Hawaii to work on sugar plantations. As the Japanese presence in America increased during the late 19th century, some Americans became alarmed. Anti-Japanese activism started in California during the 1890s and continued into the 20th century. (There was an irony here. Some leaders of opposition to Japanese immigrants were themselves immigrants – from Europe!)

In 1922, the U.S. Supreme Court ruled that Japanese could not become naturalized American citizens. In 1924, President Calvin Coolidge signed a law that stopped Japanese immigration to the U.S.**❷**

❷ This double standard applied not only to Japanese immigrants, but also to immigrants from most of Asia. The U.S. government strictly limited Asian immigration while placing almost no controls on European immigration. Most of these racist immigration policies were abandoned after World War II.

As the U.S. and Japan prepared for war in 1941, a U.S. congressman recommended putting Japanese-Americans in prison (that is, internment camps) to make sure that Japan would practice "good behavior." That was what happened. After the Japanese attack on Pearl Harbor, Japanese-Americans in Hawaii and on the U.S. mainland were rounded up and jailed.

Ten "relocation centers" housed Japanese-Americans during the war. It is worth noting that German-Americans and Italian-Americans were not sent to concentration camps in the U.S. during World War II, even though the U.S. was at war with Germany and Italy as well as Japan.

After the war, the government made a small effort to repay

Japanese-Americans for the money they lost due to official persecution during the war, but only a small amount of money was actually paid. In 1988, the U.S. passed a law to allow a $20,000 individual payment to each Japanese-American **internee** from the war years who was still living.

Japanese-Americans recovered quickly from the hardships of the war. In 1962, less than 20 years after the war ended, a Japanese-American, Daniel Inouye, was elected to the U.S. Senate from Hawaii.

Japanese-Americans were kept at the Manzanar concentration camp during World War II.

Now, Japanese-Americans are prominent in America's intellectual, political, and cultural life. They include actor George Takei (*Star Trek*), scientist Michio Kaku, and Congressman Robert Matsui from California.

📃 **WORDS FOR SOCIOLOGY**

✓ arrest
✓ hardship
✓ immigration
✓ migrant
✓ naturalize
✓ persecution
✓ prominent

Sociology

Questions

01   How did Japanese immigration to the U.S. begin, and when?

02   After what event in 1941 were Japanese-Americans in Hawaii and on the U.S. mainland rounded up and jailed?

03   Look at the word **internee** in the passage. What do you think **internee** means here?

04   The author points out several essential differences between the experiences of Japanese immigrants and those of European immigrants. Explain these differences in your own words.

4.5   The 20th Century: America's Urban Underclass

Homelessness is a large problem in the U.S.

One of the most visible problems of American cities in the late 20th century was the presence of large numbers of very poor people. These people were known as the "urban underclass." They were largely unemployed, and unemployable, because they lacked the skills and habits needed to hold regular jobs. Many of them spent their days begging for money on the streets.

Only a few years earlier, the urban underclass had not been a great problem in America. In the final years of the 20th century, however, several factors combined to make the underclass expand.

One factor was the changing character of America's work force. In a high-tech age, many jobs required skills and training that the poor did not have and could not acquire. Other factors included population growth, immigration, and economic decline. To make matters worse, the U.S. released many of the mentally ill from hospitals and other facilities❶. These people were too sick to hold jobs, yet they no longer had places to live.

❶ At that time, many mentally ill people were released because it was believed they had a right to be free, even if they were mentally ill.

The result was a huge increase in poverty and homelessness. The effects could be seen everywhere, every day. Beggars in large numbers roamed the streets and shouted for money. They rode subway trains and held out cups for coins. They wandered into restaurants and apartment buildings, seeking cash. Even a short walk downtown became an encounter with shabby men who asked, "Spare change?" Cities began to look as they had looked during the Great Depression of the 1930s.

The middle and upper classes were not sure how to deal with the underclass. Some people gave the beggars money. Others ignored them and wished they would disappear. Very few middle- and upper-class Americans took the trouble to talk with people in the underclass. Talking with them, however, was instructive. One learned more than simply that some people were very poor. One also learned how little separated the underclass from the middle class, and how easily someone from the middle class could slip and **wind up** on the bottom.

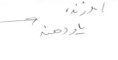

↳ finally arrive at a situation

Many beggars explained that they were once part of the middle class. But then, they dropped into the underclass when something – alcohol, drugs, divorce, or whatever – seriously hurt their incomes and their lives. Thus, they wound up on the streets, with little or no opportunity to climb back up again to middle-class status.

In principle, they could get help. But cities were rarely sympathetic to the underclass, and some made a special effort either to keep the poor out of sight or to make them go elsewhere.

📑 **WORDS FOR SOCIOLOGY**

✓ acquire
✓ disappear
✓ expand
✓ factor
✓ ignore
✓ lack
✓ presence
✓ underclass
✓ unemployed
✓ urban

Sociology

Questions

01   What caused the growth of the underclass in America?

02   Look at the expression **wind up** in the passage. What do you think **wind up** means in this context?

03   According to the author, what can be learned from talking to members of the underclass?

4.6   The 20th Century: Class Lines

Once, it was popular to see America's class structure in very simplistic terms. There were "the rich," and there were "the poor." In the 19th and 20th centuries, it became fashionable to divide American society into three classes: upper, middle, and lower, with most Americans in the middle class. This second, three-level model is still widely used.

On close examination, however, the situation starts to look more complex. The lower class has its poor members, who at least have homes to live in, and its very poor members, the so-called homeless. At the other extreme, the upper class has its merely "rich" and, far above them, the "super-rich," who have wealth so great that it is hard to comprehend.

What about the middle class? How is it divided? On the basis of income alone, one might see in it three levels (lower-middle, middle-middle, and upper-middle), or one might adopt a more complex model that includes many other factors too, such as education and property.

Here is a hypothetical example. Consider two people in the middle class. We will call them Jones and Smith.

Jones is rich in money. He has a lot of money in the bank but does not spend much of it. He lives in an ordinary apartment, drives an ordinary car, and puts his money into savings.

Now, consider his neighbor Smith. Smith has much less money in the bank, but he has a lot of land. His house sits on a big yard, and he owns land in many other places too. Unlike Jones, who is rich in money, Smith is rich in property.

If we think of class only in terms of income, Jones might be upper-middle class, and Smith might be lower-middle class. But when we consider both income and property, Smith – the relatively **cash-poor** person – might rank higher than Jones!

This simple example shows how class in America is not a simple phenomenon at all. There are different classes, to be sure. A millionaire is in a higher social class than a homeless beggar. As America's society and economy have become more complex, however, traditional class lines have become increasingly vague. Someone with a non-traditional way of life may not fit easily into any one category.

This kind of puzzle keeps sociologists busy and often leaves others confused. "Where do I fit in?" Americans ask. Most Americans see themselves as middle class❶. But where is that "middle," really? Trying to define it can be like trying to grab a cloud.

❶ This is largely because both upper class and lower class social status have some negative connotations attached to them. Many Americans associate lower class status with failure. At the same time, many Americans are suspicious of upper class status and assume that the upper class must have gotten their wealth through dishonest means. For this reason, even poor and rich Americans often describe themselves as middle class.

📑 **WORDS FOR SOCIOLOGY**

✓ adopt
✓ complex
✓ income
✓ lower class
✓ middle class
✓ phenomenon
✓ property
✓ upper class
✓ vague

Sociology

Questions

01 Look at the expression **cash-poor** in this passage. What do you think **cash-poor** means here?

02 According to the passage, why is "class" in America sometimes hard to define? Explain in your own words.

03 According to the passage, why is an understanding of their social class important to Americans?

4.7   The 20th Century: How Real Is the "American Dream"?

Horatio Alger wrote about the "American dream."

From time to time, American authors lament what they see as the death of the "American dream." In his 1971 novel *Fear and Loathing in Las Vegas*, for example, journalist Hunter Thompson describes his search for the so-called American dream. At last, the search leads him to the site of a nightclub that burned down years before. The message seems clear. The American dream died long ago.

But what was, or is, the American dream, really? Discussions of its death or survival must address that question. And the question has many answers.

Consider the "American dream" as an economic goal. For many years, the "American dream" was to achieve economic independence – that is, to become a success in business and get rich, or at least become successful enough to afford a good home. In principle, the American dream meant everyone had the opportunity to realize that goal.

Success was not guaranteed, of course, but at least the opportunity was there. American history is filled with stories of ambitious men and women who set out to achieve that dream and succeeded. Horatio Alger, the 19th-century American author of stories about success, made such "rags to riches❶" stories famous through his novels. Indeed, the American dream came to be known as a "Horatio Alger story," in which a poor boy succeeds through cleverness and hard work.

❶ *Rags to riches* is a common expression used to describe someone's ascent from poverty to wealth.

The stories were fiction, but they had enough **foundation** in fact to make the American dream of economic independence seem feasible. In the 19th and 20th centuries, many Americans made that dream come true. Even in the late 20th century, it was possible for a college dropout to become fantastically rich in the computer business❷.

❷ This refers to Bill Gates, who left college early to found Microsoft.

On a smaller scale, countless other Americans also realized more modest versions of that same dream. Poor men and women and their families planned well, worked hard, and attained a certain degree of prosperity, if not great wealth. Even if one did not reach the very top, the poor still had opportunities to climb to middle-class status. Because it was true to some extent, that dream attracted millions of immigrants to the United States.

◁》 Horatio Alger
[houréiʃiòu ǽlgər]

📑 **WORDS FOR SOCIOLOGY**

✓ afford
✓ attain
✓ attract
✓ feasible
✓ foundation
✓ guarantee
✓ independence
✓ lament
✓ prosperity
✓ status

Questions

01 Why does the author compare the American dream to a nightclub? Explain in one sentence.

02 Which 19th-century author does the passage mention, and why?

03 Look at the word **foundation** in the passage. What does **foundation** mean in this context?

04 What do you think the author's opinion of the American dream is? How do you know? Explain.

Sociology

4.8 The 20th Century: The Academic Class

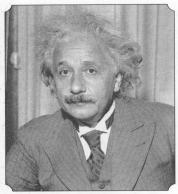

Albert Einstein is a good example of the academic class.

❶ *Ivory tower* is a figure of speech that means colleges and universities.

The "academic class" – made up of college and university professors – was once seen as a distinct part of American society. "Academics," as they were called, were thought to **dedicate** their lives to knowledge, through research and teaching.

Many Americans would have considered it wrong for a college professor to become an entertainer or merchant. Indeed, the forgetful professor, interested only in his academic subject and nothing else, and careless about everyday things, became a subject of jokes.

(Did this image, perhaps, owe something to the old story about the death of the Greek mathematician Archimedes? According to the story, he was murdered while busy with research. His last words were a request to his murderer not to disturb his work!)

Though some academics had profitable hobbies outside the academic world, such as writing popular fiction, the wall between the academic and non-academic worlds remained largely intact until the mid-1900s, when the academic world, or "ivory tower❶," found itself losing its identity – slowly at first, then quickly

By the late 20th century, the boundary between the academic class and everyone else was no longer distinct. The rise of mass media such as radio and television created an endless demand for interesting stories. Academics had countless interesting stories to tell about history, science, and even distant planets and stars.

So, the American media made stars – of a different kind – out of some academics who understood the media and knew what they wanted to hear and see. Economists, historians, and other scholars also became familiar personalities on radio and television. At least two astronomers had their own television shows!

Previously, walls (so to speak) had defined the academic class. The "television professor" represented the fall of one wall. Another wall fell to business. As big companies saw possibility for profit in scientific research, for example, some academics became well-paid advisors to businesses, or even became businessmen themselves. By the 1980s, it was nothing too unusual for a faculty member at a leading university to be the center of a corporation.

Did trends like these mean that the academic class was dying, or just changing to suit the times? Definitely, it was changing. But not everyone was happy with the changes.

📑 WORDS FOR SOCIOLOGY

✓ dedicate
✓ demand
✓ distant
✓ distinct
✓ disturb
✓ intact
✓ profitable

Sociology

Questions

01   Look at the word **dedicate** in the passage. What do you think **dedicate** means in this context?

02   The author uses two images – walls and a tower – to describe the academic world. Why does the author uses these images? Explain.

03   What factors contributed to the changes in the academic class?

4.9 The 20ᵗʰ Century: Superstar Scientists

Would Newton be a superstar scientist today... or not?

❶ Marilyn Monroe and James Dean were movie stars in the 1950s and 1960s. Elvis Presley was a famous musician at the same time. All three are commonly seen as symbols of their time.

❷ A *sound bite* is a brief statement or explanation used in an interview on radio or television.

The "superstar" – a very popular entertainer – became a familiar part of American life in the 20ᵗʰ century. Marilyn Monroe, Elvis Presley, James Dean❶, and countless other superstars became part of popular culture and everyday talk. They were known everywhere, and their names and images were worth a lot of money.

The "superstar" effect was not confined to entertainment. Superstar athletes appeared as well because the sports industry was linked closely to entertainment. There were superstar politicians, superstar diplomats, superstar authors, and even superstar cooks. With superstar status came money – sometimes, so much money that a certain superstar could become a whole industry by himself or herself.

For a long time, science resisted this trend. Scientists were seen as a different group from athletes or entertainers because they did more "serious" work. Things began to change, however, in the late 20ᵗʰ century. Media coverage of science made some scientists public figures, especially when they were reasonably good-looking and understood how the media worked. The media valued a scientist who looked good on camera and could explain things in neat "sound bites❷," or short, clear explanations. In this way, some scientists became media personalities – people the media sought out to comment on news about science.

As scientists became celebrities, their "name value" increased. They were famous. So, their names and images were worth more. They could charge more for lectures and books. They could get rich – by scientists' standards, anyway – through appearing in the media. If they were not quite as **stellar** as Presley and Monroe, then they at least brought to science a greater glamour than science had known before.

As a rule, superstar scientists were praised and admired. They made good role models for the young. Before long, however, skeptics began to wonder if the "superstar" system was good for science.

In 1993, for example, an article in the journal *The Scientist* asked if scientists would soon be represented by agents, just as top actors, actresses, and athletes are. Would publishers bid for rights to publish important scientific works? That was not too hard to imagine. It was just as easy to imagine universities bidding for top scientists. Superstar scientists could command top prices, if they wished.

But what would such a situation mean for science? Would a few glamorous figures get more money and power than they really deserved, just because they had more "name value"? How far would schools and journals go to attract superstar scientists? And how would all this affect scientists who were less famous and favored, but who were doing more important work?

◁⏽ Marilyn Monroe
[mǽrəlin mənróu]

📑 Words for Sociology

✓ affect
✓ celebrity
✓ command
✓ confine
✓ resist
✓ stellar
✓ value

Questions

01   According to the passage, what qualities do scientists need to become superstars?

02   The author writes, "They could get rich – by scientists' standards, anyway – through appearing in the media." What does the author imply about scientists and money? Explain.

03   Look at the word **stellar** in the passage. What do you think **stellar** means in this context?

04   In your own words, explain the objections some people have to scientists becoming superstars.

Sociology

4.10 The 20th Century: The Effects of Automation

In the early 20th century, filmmakers like Fritz Lang, in his movie *Metropolis*, imagined a future when humans would be slaves to machines. Lang filmed dramatic scenes of men struggling – not always successfully – to meet machines' demands. Only a few years later, such dreams appeared very close to reality.

Around the mid-20th century, America became an automated society. Technology put machines in charge of many jobs that humans had done before. Machines ran factories, to a large extent. Machines served food, sorted mail, and directed traffic. Machines even supervised other machines. In short, automation had arrived on a **grand** scale. No part of society remained unaffected.

But how exactly did this change affect American society? The effects were numerous and profound. One change was an expectation of better service and products. Automation made it possible to make products and deliver services more reliably than ever before. Thus, new and higher standards of service and product quality emerged. In other words, the public learned to expect better services and products because of automation.

How could industry and government satisfy those expectations? The answer was more automation. So, automation changed society in a way that ensured continued reliance on automation. More automation, in turn, meant still more automation ... and so on, until, by the early 1960s, Americans seriously wondered if machines would make human labor obsolete in the not-too-distant future❶.

❶ The advent and rapid spread of computers in the 1960s and 1970s heightened this sense of unease.

At the same time, automation had a more subtle – but also more troubling – effect on society. Automation gave machines authority over people in many everyday situations. Machines told humans when they might or might not move their cars, place telephone calls, and cross the street. People took orders from automated systems. That became part of life, like mild weather in spring.

It was a good arrangement, as long as the machines worked as they were meant to work. But what would happen if the machines failed? A malfunction might create a mess that humans would be helpless to correct. One science fiction story of the early 1960s, for example, imagined a day when all the traffic lights in a city turned green at once. The resulting traffic jam could be imagined. It would paralyze a city.

What if all the traffic lights in a city turned green at once?

Of course, automated systems existed to prevent such events, or at least to make them very unlikely. But that did not alter an unpleasant reality. As humans surrendered authority to machines, people became relatively powerless.

The question, then, naturally came to mind: who was serving whom? Were machines serving people, or were people serving machines? The fantasies of filmmakers in the 1920s were becoming fact, and in almost as dramatic a fashion.

🔊 Fritz Lang [frits læŋ]

📑 **Words for Sociology**

✓ alter
✓ effect
✓ emerge
✓ grand
✓ malfunction
✓ numerous
✓ paralyze
✓ profound
✓ reliance

Sociology

Q u e s t i o n s

01 In your own words, explain the negative effects automation has had on American society.

02 Look at the word **grand** in the passage. What do you think **grand** means here?

large huge

03 Explain in your own words how Americans' concerns about technology have been reflected in movies and in science fiction.

4.11 The 20th Century: Conformists and Rebels

In America, James Dean's name is basically synonymous with "rebel."

❶ To *come along* means to appear or to arrive.

❷ To *burn oneself out* means to use all of one's energies. It is commonly used in situations when people lead a wild or reckless lifestyle.

American society always has had its rebels, who wanted to go their own way, and its conformists, who wanted to be like the majority. In more than 200 years of U.S. history, the rebel has taken many forms. Every decade or two in the 20th century, a new kind of rebel came along❶.

In the 1950s, the "teenage rebel" became a cultural hero in the United States. Figures like actor James Dean stood for the young, lonely rebel against the rest of society. During the early 1960s, for example, folk singers rebelled against the conformism of the 1950s. The singers made fun of a society where everyone was expected to look and behave exactly the same.

In entertainment during the late 1960s and early 1970s, the rebel took the form of a young person on a journey, in some cases across the vast U.S. itself, in search of some better way of life. Sometimes the journey ended in success, and sometimes it ended in failure or even tragedy, as the rebel exhausted himself or was killed.

But whenever a rebel emerged, his **heyday** did not last long. Soon, he became too familiar and lost the public's attention. Then he faded away, and the conformist – a conservative, comparatively boring figure – took his place. Rebellion could be fun, but "going along with the crowd" was usually safer.

This was not surprising. Though the conformists and rebels were opposites and appeared to be enemies, they actually were partners and needed each other. How could one have rebellion without a society of conformists against which to rebel? And what would conformists do without rebels who burned themselves out❷ and thus showed the futility of rebellion?

That strange pattern – apparent enemies who are really partners – is essential to the cultural history of the U.S. This is because popular culture is basically drama, and drama is a story of conflict. To have conflict, one must have opposing points of view – conformist versus rebel, dreamer versus realist, or whatever.

So, the opponents need each other. Otherwise, there is no conflict, and one has no story to tell. Though conflicts in American popular culture do not always occur in a moral setting – good versus evil, hero versus villain – they are especially lively when they do so. To make the best entertainment, however, the characters should not be absolutes. The villain should have good points, and the hero should have flaws.

In similar fashion, the conformist should have something of the rebel in him, and vice versa. Each character then sees a little of himself in the other, and the story becomes much more interesting.

📃 **WORDS FOR SOCIOLOGY**

✓ apparent
✓ conflict
✓ emerge → come out, arise
✓ essential
✓ flaw → عیب, نقص
✓ futility → عبثی، بے فائدگی، بیکاری
✓ heyday
✓ rebel
✓ vast → وسیع، جسیم، نہایت

Sociology

Questions

01 According to the passage, what are some of the characteristics of the "rebel" in American pop cuture?

02 Look at the word **heyday** in the passage. What do you think **heyday** means in this context?

03 In your own words, explain how the concepts of the rebel and the conformist are dependent on each other.

4.12 The 20th Century: The 1960s Counterculture

● The mid to late 1960s were a time of tremendous social upheaval in America, with the civil rights movement and opposition to the Vietnam War prompting many young Americans to question the values of their parents' generation.

Starting around the year 1965●, a new social movement appeared among young people in the United States. In general, it was known as the "counterculture." The prefix "counter" means "against," and the counterculture was against America's dominant culture of the time.

The dominant culture was basically conservative in lifestyle, speech, and dress. Its characteristics included short hair and clean-shaven faces on men, restrained behavior, and almost uniform clothing.

Members of the counterculture tried their best not to look or act like their parents.

The counterculture, by contrast, had a more colorful style. "Counterculturists" dressed oddly and spoke in strange slang. They held unpopular views. The men grew beards and wore their hair long. In short, people in the counterculture had habits which shocked the rest of society. What is more, they did not merely practice these things. They actually dared the rest of society to stop them!

That, at least, was how the conservative majority saw the counterculture. Things looked different, of course, from the other side. People in the counterculture thought they were merely seeking "freedom." That was, after all, what Americans celebrated every July 4. Freedom was what America valued most highly, wasn't it? So, the counterculture saw no need to wear ties, get short haircuts, and behave in traditional ways. "Do your own thing●" was their motto. In other words, they wanted to be unusual and creative, not identical and unoriginal.

❷ *Do your own thing* is a slang expression which means do what you want.

The situation really was more complex than this. There were many different groups within the counterculture. Some were closer to traditional thought and behavior than others. Some believed in moving away from the rest of society. Others thought they should try to change the rest of society. Some parts of the counterculture were gentle and peace-loving. Others were loud and offensive.

Still, they all looked much different from American society in the 1950s and early 1960s, and the change was much greater than a mere difference of opinions between generations. The older generation of the 1960s had worked hard within a strict social order to make America the most successful and richest nation in the world. If the result was a bland society, they thought, then that was a small price to pay for success and prosperity.

Young Americans in the counterculture, however, had a different view – or did they? What the hippies and other "counterculturists" said was not necessarily what they really believed. They might say "Do your own thing," but in many cases they actually meant, "Conform to the **norm**." The counterculture had social rules that were just as rigid as the older generation's. And like the older generation, they looked down on those who did not agree with their norms of behavior. Their norm just happened to be different from that of their parents.

📑 **WORDS FOR SOCIOLOGY**

✓ conform
✓ conservative
✓ counterculture
✓ dominant
✓ generation
✓ lifestyle
✓ majority
✓ norm
✓ offensive

Questions

01 In you own words, explain what the counterculture was.

02 Explain the differences in how the older generation and the younger generation viewed the counterculture.

03 Look at the word **norm** in the passage. What do you think **norm** means in this context?

04 What point is the author trying to make in the final paragraph? Explain in your own words.

Sociology

The 20ᵗʰ Century: Schools – What Do You Get for Your Money?

a mounts of money

What does college tuition really buy?

Americans spend great **sums** on education. A year of study at a leading college or university may cost $30,000 or more. That is a lot of money. In general, it buys "an education." But what, more exactly, does it buy? Let us look at an imaginary example.

Here is a large university in the eastern United States. It has a good reputation and famous professors on its faculty. It is very wealthy. It is known all around the world. Tuition here is high. A four-year degree costs more than $120,000. That is more than two years' income for an average American family.

This is not a school, however, for "average" students. Many of its graduates are rich and powerful, or at least leaders in their fields of work. They are well-known lawyers, politicians, authors, entertainers, and scientists. A degree from this school, then, means prestige. People pay attention when you mention its name.

On close examination, however, the school's great reputation is puzzling. Look at its undergraduate programs. They are about the same as those at other, less famous schools. Those other schools teach the same subjects, just as well. Yet their prestige is lower, and they charge less money for a degree.

What makes this school so prestigious and expensive? What is special about it? How can it charge so much for the same knowledge that other schools provide for less money?

Some people might reply, "That is because it is a great school!" There is, however, a more specific explanation. The school has prestige – and high tuition – because it also sells access to networks.

These are not computer networks (though the school has plenty of those too). Instead, they are social and professional networks❶. Here, you do not meet ordinary students and faculty. You meet well-connected people who are, or someday will be, important. Knowing those people is worth a lot of money.

The school's tuition, then, buys more than just knowledge and training. It also buys entry to a wealthy and important class in society. That is what prestige means in this case. If you go to this school, you meet people who can be very useful later in your career. You get networks. Through them, you can get wealth and prestige. That, more than anything else, is what your money buys. And many people think the expense is justified. After all, not just anyone can join a famous club.

❶ These networks are sometimes called old boys networks. A good example of such a system would be the Citadel, a prestigious military college in South Carolina. Much of the political and business structure of the American South is controlled by graduates of the Citadel. Graduates who already hold positions of power often help younger graduates attain powerful positions.

 WORDS FOR SOCIOLOGY

✓ expense
✓ income
✓ justify
✓ prestige
✓ reputation
✓ tuition

Sociology

Questions

01 In your own words, explain why Americans pay such high tuition fees to attend top universities.

02 Look at the word **sums** in the passage. What do you think **sums** means here?

4.14 The 20ᵗʰ-21ˢᵗ Century: Who Should Pay for Public Schools?

Americans often complain about their public schools and the quality of education children get there. Many times, these complaints reflect one of the oldest and deepest divisions in American society: the rich versus the poor.

Look at U.S. public schools, and you will see great differences among them. Some are big and well-equipped. Students there do very well. Other schools, however, are poor and run-down. They do not have enough supplies. Their buildings are old and falling apart. Students there do poorly.

In some places, where rich towns sit next to poor towns, schools only a short distance apart will be **worlds apart** in quality. How does this happen? To find one answer, look at where money for public schools comes from.

In the United States, localities – that is, cities and counties – are responsible for funding their public schools❶. Money for schools comes mostly from taxes on property. Taxes collected by a local government are used to fund schools, among many other things. This system has worked in the U.S. for many years. But is it fair?

That depends on how one defines "fair." Some people say it is not fair because schools in wealthy communities get more money than schools in poor communities. The rich communities, then, can afford better schools than the poor ones.

Some people think this problem should be corrected by the "Robin Hood❷" method: take from the rich and give to the poor. But would it be fair to take money from rich communities and use it for schools in poor communities? Should taxpayers in Town A be

❶ Public schools receive their entire funding in this manner, and there is no tuition for public schools in America.

❷ Robin Hood is a legendary British thief who stole from the rich and gave the money to the poor.

forced to support schools in Town B, even if schools in Town B are very needy? To put it another way: why should anyone be forced to pay for someone else's schools?

There are many suggestions for solving this problem. One is to find another way of funding schools. Maybe schools should be funded from a state lottery or statewide tax instead of property taxes. That might make more money available for poor schools.

But then, the "fairness" issue returns. A statewide tax to support schools would put an unequal burden on taxpayers. Some would still have to pay more than their share. Reformers say, "Poor schools need more money!" But taxpayers say, "Don't tax us for them!" Who is right? And which part of "the public" should pay for improving public schools? There is no clear answer, nor is one likely to appear soon.

Maybe children are the future, as the saying goes. But partly because of the U.S. social structure, there is great resistance to change in funding public schools – even in the very good cause of improving education.

WORDS FOR SOCIOLOGY

✓ afford
✓ available
✓ community
✓ fund
✓ improve
✓ property
✓ quality
✓ support

Questions

01   What is this passage mainly about? Summarize it in one sentence.

02   Look at the expression **worlds apart** in the passage. What do you think **worlds apart** means in this context?

03   What causes the differences between public schools in America?

04   What possible solutions does the author suggest to solve these problems?

Sociology

4.15 The 20th-21st Century: A Society on Drugs

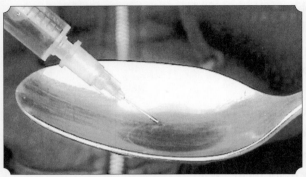

Illegal drug usage is a large and persistent problem in the U.S.

The "drug culture" is nothing new in the United States. Since colonial times, Americans have used drugs to change their moods. Alcohol and narcotics were once widely sold in the form of "patent medicines," or medicines that could be bought in stores without a doctor's prescription. These fake "medicines" did not really cure anything. They only made the user feel better.

❶ The Volstead Act made alcohol illegal from 1919 to 1931.

From time to time, the U.S. has tried to restrain its drug culture. In the early 20th century, for example, Prohibition tried to restrict the production and sale of alcohol❶. Prohibition was not effective. Americans kept drinking anyway. Prohibition also led to the rise of gangsters like Al Capone, who got rich by supplying alcohol illegally.

In general, American attempts to curtail drug use have failed. Illegal drugs became so popular in the 20th century that the "drug economy" – that is, the sale and purchase of illegal drugs – did much to support the economy of some American cities. The expression "recreational drugs," meaning drugs taken just for fun, entered the American language.

So did the expression "designer drugs," meaning new drugs invented to be taken for pleasure. In the 1980s, a whole industry arose to make and distribute designer drugs. This industry took advantage of a **loophole** in the law.

an ineffective part of a law

The law could prohibit making and using a particular drug. But if a certain drug was not banned specifically, then the police could not stop it. So, chemists would "tweak," or slightly modify, an existing drug to make it into something new. It still had a strong effect, but its use could not be stopped unless lawmakers passed a new law specifically against it.

At the same time, American society was also flooded with prescription drugs that changed the user's moods. These drugs were part of the great revolution in medicine that took place in the second half of the 20th century, when new drugs came into use for treatment of mental illness and other conditions.

❷ *Drugged out* is a slang term which describes a person who has taken too many drugs and is no longer able to think in a proper manner.

There was no law against using these drugs, and one could get them easily. Sometimes a doctor's prescription was not even needed. Especially common were tranquillizers, drugs meant to make the user calm and relaxed. Some pain relievers were also in great demand because they had a powerful effect on the user's mood.

🔊 **Al Capone** [æl kəpóun]

By the end of the 20th century, then, America had become a "drugged-out❷" society. Almost everyone, it seemed, was taking one mood-changing drug or another, legal or illegal. At times, the U.S. looked like a giant experiment to see how drugged ("stoned," in American slang) a society could get and still survive.

📑 **WORDS FOR SOCIOLOGY**

✓ advantage
✓ ban
✓ curtail
✓ distribute
✓ effective
✓ fake
✓ illegal
✓ loophole
✓ prescription
✓ prohibit
✓ restrain
✓ restrict

Sociology

Questions

01　Why does the author mention gangster Al Capone in the passage?

02　Look at the word **loophole** in the passage. What do you think **loophole** means here?

03　Why has the U.S. found it difficult to stop drug usage?

4.16   The 21ˢᵗ Century: Los Angeles Ignites

The Los Angeles riots were the worst riots in U.S. history.

❶ The civil rights movement aimed to have legal rights guaranteed for all citizens, including African-Americans.

❷ A *verdict* is a jury's decision – guilty or not guilty – in a trial. A *sentence,* such as time in jail, is a judge's decision.

By the 1990s, most Americans believed that their nation's history of racial tension and unrest was a thing of the past. Since the civil rights movement of the 1960s**❶**, they felt they had been making steady progress towards an equal society in which the color of one's skin was not a factor. By the early 1990s, many Americans believed they now lived in such a society. That belief was shattered on April 29, 1992, when the city of Los Angeles exploded in flame.

The Los Angeles riot of 1992 was arguably the worst race riot the nation had ever experienced. Over three days of rioting, over 50 people were killed and thousands more were injured. By the time the fires were put out, 8,000 buildings had been destroyed or damaged by fire, amounting to over $1 billion in property damage. As the smoke cleared, Americans were left dazed and wondering what had just happened.

On the surface, the riots seemed to be about the trial of four L.A. police officers. In 1991, a man with a video camera taped a group of four white police officers severely beating an African-American man, Rodney King. The police claimed that King had been resisting arrest and that they were simply using force to arrest him. However, after viewing the tape, which was played repeatedly on national television, many Americans found this story **hard to swallow**.

The four officers were put on trial for the beating of Rodney King, and it was widely expected that they would be found guilty. However, when the verdict**❷** was read (again on national television),

the jury ruled that three of the officers were innocent of all charges.
News of the verdict quickly spread, and Los Angeles burned.

A look at the riots suggests that there was far more at work than
simple anger over the King verdict. Police brutality, especially
towards young African-American men, had been a fact of life in Los
Angeles for quite a while. Furthermore, the economic differences
between the rich and the poor, which existed in all American cities,
were present in an extreme form in Los Angeles, and were largely
drawn along racial lines.

One only had to compare the incredibly rich (and almost entirely
white) areas like Beverly Hills and the desperately poor area of
South Central (mostly African-American) Los Angeles to see the
glaring differences that existed. So, when an all-white jury found
three white police officers not guilty of beating an African-
American man, it was not the cause of the riots. It was simply the
match that ignited the fire.

WORDS FOR SOCIOLOGY

✓ explode
✓ factor
✓ ignite
✓ innocent
✓ racial
✓ riot
✓ steady
✓ tension
✓ unrest
✓ verdict

Questions

01 What did the 1992 Los Angeles riot show Americans about their society?

02 What does the author seem to suggest about the role of television in the riot? How do you know?

03 Look at the phrase **hard to swallow** in the passage. What do you think **hard to swallow** means in this context?

04 According to the author, what caused the L.A. riot? What role did the King verdict play?

Sociology

4.17 The 21ˢᵗ Century: **Is the "Melting Pot" an Illusion?**

Americans like to think that all immigrants will "melt" into American culture over time.

❶ Early immigrants to the U.S., when the idea of the melting pot was formed, came largely from Europe and shared fundamental cultural values with existing Americans.

❷ To *take up* means to accept, follow, or adopt. Here, *up* is used as an adverb.

❸ *Hispanics* are people from Spanish-speaking American countries like Mexico.

America is sometimes described as a "melting pot." Imagine a giant pot in which different metals are melted and mixed together to make something new. That is how some people used to see America. They thought people from many different countries would come to America, mix together, and form a new people. In principle, Irish, Germans, Scots, Spanish, Norwegians, French, Italians, and other immigrants would become a new people – Americans – with new characteristics.

To some extent, that was what happened. Some "melting" and mixing took place. But some groups were much harder to "melt" and mix than others. In fact, some of them resisted melting completely! They did not mix with the rest of the population. Instead, they remained separate.

There were many reasons. For example, some immigrants had customs and ways of life that were fundamentally different from the traditional Protestant, European culture of the U.S.❶ They found it hard to take up❷ a new way of living. They wanted to keep their old ways. This did not mean they were ineligible to become Americans, but it meant that the image of a "melting pot" did not really describe America very well. A quilt or salad made a better comparison! In the late 20ᵗʰ century, the great influx of Hispanics❸ to the U.S., largely from Mexico, made that fact plain to see.

By the year 2005, almost one-third of the people in the state of California were Hispanics. In Texas, the population was more than one-fourth Hispanic. This sparked intense debate in these states about just what it meant to be "American."

In part, this was because the Spanish-speaking immigrants did not mix easily with the rest of the population. Their Hispanic culture remained their own. They did not want to mix or be "melted." They wanted to remain as they were, even while living within American borders.

Why? Some Hispanic immigrants in the late 20th century considered the U.S. a decadent and immoral society based on pursuit of money and sex. Also, Americans could seem arrogant, cold, and unfriendly. Was a culture like that really worth joining?

So, America in the early 21st century already had become two separate nations (if not three or four or more), in a sense, because the "melting pot" model had failed. It was an illusion. Some immigrants would not be absorbed or **assimilated**. They refused to "melt." So, the challenge for America in the 21st century would be to find a way to accommodate several very different definitions of just what is meant to be American.

📑 WORDS FOR SOCIOLOGY

- ✓ absorb
- ✓ accommodate
- ✓ assimilate
- ✓ custom
- ✓ describe
- ✓ illusion
- ✓ immoral
- ✓ ineligible
- ✓ influx
- ✓ resist

Questions

01 In your own words, explain the concept of America as a melting pot.

02 What problems does the melting pot model of American society have?

03 Look at the word **assimilated** in the passage. What do you think **assimilated** means in this context?

to become a part of another culture and fully mix into that new culture

04 What are some the reasons cited in the passage for why some immigrants may not wish to assimilate into American culture?

Sociology

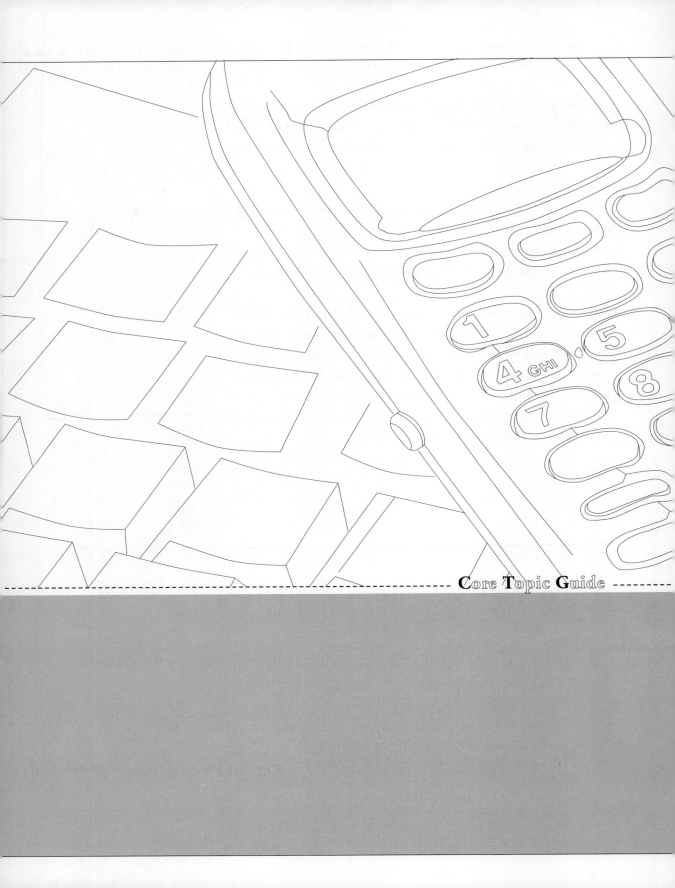

SOCIAL SCIENCES V

Communications

5.1 The 19th-21st Century: "Ameringlish" vs. "Britglish"

Restrooms in America are called water closets in Britain. This is just one example of the differences in the English language.

❶ Shaw was a famous Irish playwright and social critic in the early 1900s.

More than just an ocean separates Britain from the United States. Although they both speak the English language, there are many differences between English as it is spoken in the United States (that is, "Ameringlish") and as it is spoken in Britain ("Britglish"). Author George Bernard Shaw❶ made a famous remark about this difference. He said the British and Americans were separated by the language they had in common!

Shaw was joking, but he made an important point. Sometimes British and American speakers of English have trouble understanding each other, because Ameringlish and Britglish have **diverged** in many ways during the last 200 years.

Vocabulary, for example, can differ greatly on opposite sides of the Atlantic Ocean. In the U.S., "dear" means "beloved." In Britain, however, it means "expensive." Americans drive "trucks," but the British drive "lorries." In America, a car has a "hood," whereas in Britain it has a "bonnet." Other car-related words also differ. Americans talk about a car's "trunk," but the British say "boot" instead.

Verb conjugations differ, too. The past participle of "to get," for example, is "gotten" in the U.S. and "got" in Britain. The simple past form of many verbs is another point of difference. The British often use a irregular form when Americans would use a regular form instead. "Learned" in American usage, for example, would be "learnt" in British usage, and "smelled" would be "smelt."

Still another difference is the spelling of certain words. Americans sometimes prefer a simpler spelling and will drop a letter from a British spelling. The British word "colour," for example, is spelled "color" in America, and a sense of "humour" in Britain would be a sense of "humor" in the U.S.

These are just a few ways in which the British and Americans speak and write differently. Of course, both countries speak English. But after English was transplanted to America hundreds of years ago, the American branch of English developed in its own unique way!

◁» Ameringlish [ǽmərínɡliʃ]
◁» Britglish [brítɡliʃ]
◁» George Bernard Shaw
[dʒɔːrdʒ bərnáːrd ʃɔː]

📑 WORDS FOR COMMUNICATIONS

✓ diverge
✓ irregular
✓ regular
✓ separate
✓ transplant
✓ unique

Questions

01 What are two ways in which American English and British English differ? Give two examples from the passage.

02 Look at the word **diverged** in the passage. What do you think **diverged** means in this context?

03 What is the author's purpose in this passage? Explain in your own words.

5.2 The 20ᵗʰ-21ˢᵗ Century: The Decline of the Letter

The letter is not what it used to be.

If an American from the 18ᵗʰ or 19ᵗʰ century could visit the U.S. today, the visitor might ask, "Where have letters gone?" That is a good question. The letter plays a much less important role in the U.S. than it once did.

There was a time when the only way to communicate over long distances was by letter. Back then, before the invention of the telegraph and telephone, people spent much time actually writing letters on paper to one another.

Letters written long ago are important to historians. Some old letters reveal much about everyday life long ago: what people ate, how they worked and traveled, and what they did for recreation. Letters written long ago show that some "modern" concerns are not so modern after all. From George Washington's letters, for example, we learn that he had trouble with a newspaper subscription!

In the 18ᵗʰ century, Thomas Jefferson, author of the Declaration of Independence, sent and received great numbers of letters. He and John Adams (who worked with him on the Declaration of Independence) exchanged many letters late in their lives. Those letters make up an important part of the two men's writing.

Some novels in the 19ᵗʰ century were even written in the form of letters from one character in the story to another. This method may seem strange and awkward to readers today, who are not used to writing and reading letters. To readers in the 1800s, however, the letter form made novels seem more interesting and realistic.

In short, letters were an important form of communication in America for a long time. The telephone, however, changed all that. It let people speak with each other directly over long distances. So, it was no longer necessary to write letters. A telephone call was quicker and worked just as well. At that point, the letter began a long, slow decline in America.

By the end of the 20th century, that decline had become a **free fall**. The invention of email made it possible to send electronic messages around the world in an instant. Hardly anyone sat down to write letters on paper and put them in the mail any longer.

Suddenly, an important resource for historians was gone. A letter written on paper might last for hundreds of years and help historians long after it was written. Email, by contrast, was deleted almost as soon as it was received. But that was only one sad effect of the letter's decline.

📰 **WORDS FOR COMMUNICATIONS**

✓ decline
✓ invention
✓ realistic
✓ resource
✓ reveal
✓ subscription

Questions

01   The author mentions two reasons for the decline of the letter. Name these reasons.

02   Why are letters important to historians?

03   Look at the expression **free fall** in the passage. What do you think **free fall** means in this context?

5.3   The 20th Century: The Video Age Begins

This machine started a new era.

When the first television sets appeared in American homes during the 1950s, it was hard to imagine that this strange-looking box would change American culture from top to bottom in a few short years. Yet that is what happened. TV brought a profusion of pictures into the home, with a dramatic effect on the way Americans received and processed information.

Traditionally, communication in America was based on words. People got most of their news through words – during personal conversations, by reading newspapers and magazines, and later by listening to radio. Words carried information, and information traveled on words.

The early days of electronic communications did nothing to alter that situation. Even as radio carried speeches and entertainment all the way across the U.S., it was still unmistakably a word-based medium. To reach people in the pre-television era, you had to put something not only into words, but also into the right words.

But television changed the rules. Now, information was not limited to words. It also could be conveyed by images with tremendous effectiveness. Almost overnight, the video age arrived.

Well, you may ask, hadn't Hollywood ushered in the video age many years before, with motion pictures? That was true, in a sense. Movies were brilliant at using images to convey and reinforce their messages. But movies were different from TV, in much the same way that a single raindrop is different from a rainstorm.

The motion picture, you see, was just an occasional experience. One went to movies perhaps once a week for a couple of hours. That was because one had to visit a movie theater to see them. In those days, there was no video input directly to one's living room at home. To really be **immersed** in movies, then, one had to spend much time at the theater. *surrounded by something*

Television, though, let viewers watch images for hours ... then still more hours. Soon, Americans were awash, so to speak, in video. TV made video a pervasive part of American life.

The public's appetite for this new medium seemed boundless. People wanted more television, all the time. The flickering, black-and-white images on the home screen captivated Americans, who could not get enough of them. A whole generation of children came to be known as "television babies."

The outcome was to shift Americans' thinking away from words and toward images, in a way that no one had ever experienced before – and to make the American mind in 1960 far removed from what it had been in 1940.

📑 **WORDS FOR COMMUNICATIONS**

✓ alter
✓ appetite
✓ awash
✓ captivate
✓ convey
✓ effect
✓ immerse
✓ medium
✓ pervasive
✓ profusion
✓ reinforce
✓ tremendous
✓ usher

Questions

01 How does the author think television differed from motion pictures?

02 Look at the word **immersed** in the passage. What do you think **immersed** means in this context?

03 Look at the highlighted sentence in this passage. What does it mean, and what does it tell you about effective communication in the days before television? Based on this, what can you infer about the effect of communications after the advent of television?

5.4 The 20ᵗʰ Century: Spanglish

❶ *Spanglish* is a combination of two languages, Spanish and English.

In a multicultural nation like the United States, more than one language is spoken. The dominant language in the U.S. – English – is widely spoken alongside other languages such as Spanish. The result, in this case, is a "hybrid" language called "Spanglish❶."

Spanglish uses elements of both Spanish and English. An **oral** language rather than a written language, Spanglish is used mostly by the Hispanic population of the United States, although Spanglish occurs elsewhere too, in places such as in Panama.

Scholars do not like to use the word "Spanglish" because it sounds childish. But the name, like the language, remains in widespread use. Listen to radio stations along the U.S.-Mexican border, and you will hear Spanglish spoken all the time.

How does Spanglish form? It is a complex process. Many different kinds of "blending" work together to turn Spanish and English into Spanglish.

There is "code switching," or switching from one language to another. Here, someone who speaks both languages may switch from one to the other, talking in English for a while, then Spanish, then English again. More common is "calquing," where a word from one language gets used in the other, but in a different form.

The English word "ketchup," for example, got adopted into Spanglish as "cachu." Computers and "la Internet" have their own Spanglish vocabulary too. The English word "e-mail," in Spanglish, becomes "e-meiliar." And who are the people who hand out advertising flyers on the street? Those are "flyeros"!

Though Spanglish even has dictionaries now, it is not really a uniform language. It has many varieties. Spanglish spoken in Texas is not the same as Spanglish spoken in New York City. Moreover, there are Americans who do not like to hear Spanglish spoken at all! They think English should be English, and Spanish should be Spanish.

But languages rarely exist in such pure form. Wherever two languages are spoken in close proximity by large numbers of people, some mixing is bound to occur. So, there is a whole family of "lishes" now. Chinese and English blended to form "Chinglish," Korean and English gave rise to "Konglish," and so on.

Spanglish, then, is just another example of how English is changing – and being changed by – other major languages.

◁)) cachu [kǽtʃuː]
◁)) calquing [kǽlkwiŋ]
◁)) flyeros [flɑiérouz]
◁)) Spanglish [spǽŋgliʃ]

📑 WORDS FOR COMMUNICATIONS
✓ adopt
✓ blend
✓ hybrid
✓ multicultural
✓ oral
✓ proximity
✓ widespread

Questions

01   In your own words, explain the concept of "calquing".

02   Look at the word **oral** in the passage. What do you think **oral** means here?

03   The author mentions two "lish" languages besides Spanglish in this passage. Which are they? Where would you expect to find these languages spoken?

The 20th Century: Communication by Song

One of the most powerful lessons of 20th-century America was that songs are great persuaders. Author Zelda Fitzgerald once described people who lived according to the ideas in popular songs. What does her remark tell us? Even in the early 1900s, when she was writing, the American popular song – its message spread and amplified by the mass media – was already established as a potent tool of propaganda❶.

❶ Here, *propaganda* means misleading or biased information.

Of course, songs have always been influential in America. Among the most familiar legacies of America's wars – the Revolutionary War, the War Between the States❷, et cetera – have been its songs, from "Yankee Doodle" to "When Johnny Comes Marching Home."

❷ The War Between the States is a another name for the Civil War, which was fought from 1861-1865.

In the 20th century, however, new inventions such as the phonograph and radio gave songs a much greater power to inform and persuade the public. Recordings made it possible to reproduce songs almost anywhere without the need for an orchestra, band, or chorus. Radio went even further and allowed songs to reach around the world, carrying their messages with them.

As the broadcast media expanded in the middle years of the 20th century, so did the audience for songs and their messages. As the messages of songs gained a wider audience, and thus more power, some people began to question whether that power was such a good thing. Some people claimed that songs with negative or socially unacceptable messages were influencing people in the wrong way.

An excellent example of this controversy would be when the hip-hop star Ice-T released a song titled "Cop Killer" in 1992. The song tells the story of a man who becomes **fed up** with the brutality of police and seeks revenge. The song caused outrage in America. Police around the nation, claiming the song would inspire violence towards them, protested in front of record stores selling the album.

Vice President Dan Quayle even went on national television to speak against the song.

Ice-T's supporters were just as strong in their defense of him. They claimed that his song was protected under the freedom of speech and that it presented an important issue in society, the deep anger and mistrust many young people felt for the police.

Eventually, Ice-T removed the song from his album, but not before it had revealed a long simmering debate in American society: What effect do songs have on people, and what responsibility do musicians have for the lyrics of their songs? That debate is still going on today. Although the figures in the debate have changed, (substitute Eminem for Ice-T as America's favorite bad guy), the issue itself has come no further towards resolution.

Not everyone approves of the ideas communicated in some songs.

🔊 Dan Quayle [dæn kweil]
🔊 Zelda Fitzgerald
[zéldə fitsdʒérəld]

📄 **Words for Communications**

✓ brutality
✓ controversy
✓ establish
✓ influential
✓ inform
✓ inspire
✓ outrage
✓ persuade
✓ potent
✓ release
✓ reproduce
✓ revenge

Q u e s t i o n s

01 Why does the author mention a famous author at the beginning of this passage? Explain.

02 Look at the expression **fed up** in the passage. What do you think **fed up** means in this context?

So frustrated

03 In your own words, explain the controversy over Ice-T's song. What were the claims of the song's opponents? What were the claims of its supporters?

5.6 The 20th Century: The Internet and Language

The Internet is reshaping language.

The Internet has affected almost everything else about American society, from shopping to schoolwork. So, it comes as no surprise that the Internet has affected the American language too. In a very few years, the **conventions** of Internet use have had a big effect on the way Americans use their language.

One change is a new reliance on abbreviations, acronyms, and substitutions. Conversations online substitute "BRB" for "I'll be right back" and "LOL" for "laugh out loud." Sometimes numbers and single letters substitute for complete words. The infinitive "to be" becomes "2 b," for example, and "for you" is condensed into "4 u."

The result is a strange, often puzzling language that has been called "haxor-speak." The name "haxor-speak" is derived from the expression "hacker," which was invented in the 1980s to describe people who were very skilled at using computers. "Haxor-speak," then, is the language that "hackers," or the computer-adept, use.

A weird set of variations on familiar American usage, haxor-speak is reshaping language and communication in America. Language Americans use online, in a chat room or when sending email, is very different from standard, written language.

Haxor-speak can interfere with communication because not everyone understands it yet. Someone unfamiliar with haxor-speak vocabulary may have trouble reading an email message because the message resembles a puzzle with letters, numbers, and words ("2 good 2 b 4gotten").

Is haxor-speak a fad, a problem, or the future of the American language? The answer depends on your point of view. People who defend traditional language dislike haxor-speak and discourage its use.

Other people prefer haxor-speak because it is easier to use than standard language and can convey a lot of information in a very short space. Which is easier to type: "IMHO" or "in my humble opinion"? Haxor-speak can save time without altering the meaning of a message.

Those qualities make haxor-speak useful to students. Using the abbreviations of haxor-speak, they find it easier to take notes in class than when using ordinary language.

Whether one approves of it or not, the use of haxor-speak is becoming widespread, if not formally accepted. N a few years, do u think will it b used 4 messages 2 every1?

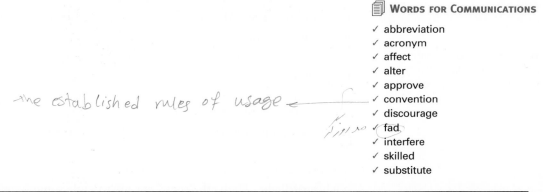

📋 **WORDS FOR COMMUNICATIONS**

✓ abbreviation
✓ acronym
✓ affect
✓ alter
✓ approve
✓ convention
✓ discourage
✓ fad
✓ interfere
✓ skilled
✓ substitute

the established rules of usage

Questions

01 According to the passage, how did the name "haxor-speak" originate? Explain in one sentence.

02 Look at the word **conventions** in the passage. What do you think **conventions** means in this context?

03 What are some advantages and disadvantages of using haxor-speak? Name two that are mentioned in the passage.

04 Why does the author include the last sentence of this passage? Explain.

5.7   The 20ᵗʰ Century: **American Slang**

From "aerospew" to "zilch," the American language is full of colorful slang, or words and expressions outside standard vocabulary. Slang originates on the "fringes" of the language, so to speak – where people invent new words for special purposes. In time, slang may find its way into everyday, "mainstream" speech. Expressions like "hacker," meaning a computer expert, were once slang but now are part of mainstream usage.

Sometimes, slang takes an ordinary word and puts it in a new context. Consider "suit," for example. In ordinary usage, it means a man's business suit – the kind of clothes a professional or executive wears to the office. But in American slang, "suit" means such a person. "He's a suit❶" means that someone is an executive or professional.

Other slang expressions originate when two words, prefixes, or suffixes are joined together in a new way. Here is an example.

The prefix "aero" means in or about the air, as in "aeronautics," the science of flight. The verb "spew" means to emit something very fast and in large amounts. As a noun, "spew" means whatever is emitted that way.

Together, they became the noun "aerospew," meaning a lot of talk without any **substance** – in other words, empty, meaningless speech. Someone might say, "He gave a talk but didn't really say anything. It was all just aerospew." (A generation or two ago, someone would have said, "It was all just hot air❷.")

At the other end of the alphabet, "zilch" means nothing, nonexistence, or something worthless. "I've got zilch" means "I have no money." To say that something is worthless or absent, one says, "It's zilch." The word "zip" has much the same meaning. A person without money might say, "I've got zip." Also, "zip" may mean a

❶ Calling someone a *suit* also carries the connotation that the person is boring or "uncool."

❷ *Hot air* is an older slang expression with the same meaning as aerospew.

score of zero on a test or examination: "What score did you get?" "Zip!"

In some cases, ordinary words with two opposite meanings may have the same meaning in slang. "Cool" and "hot" are good examples. In ordinary speech, they mean two extremes of temperature. As slang expressions, however, they both mean something is fashionable, sophisticated, or highly approved.

If a song is very popular, someone might say either "It's cool!" or "It's hot!" to describe its success. The meaning here is the same, although "cool" and "hot" ordinarily are opposite in meaning.

Americans are constantly reinventing their language. Slang is one way they do so. One never knows what will come out of this great word factory next!

◁)) aerospew [ɛ́ərouspjùː]
◁)) zilch [ziltʃ]

📑 WORDS FOR COMMUNICATIONS
✓ generation
✓ mainstream
✓ opposite
✓ ordinary
✓ originate
✓ slang

Questions

01 The passage mentions several examples of American slang. Name two examples and explain what they mean.

02 The passage explains several ways in which slang expressions are created. Explain two of them in your own words.

03 Look at the word **substance** in the passage. What do you think **substance** means in this context?

5.8   The 20ᵗʰ-21ˢᵗ Century: Acro., Abbr., & Everyday Speech

President John F. Kennedy was known as "JFK."

One **curious** element of everyday English in American usage is the large number of abbreviations (abbr.) and acronyms❶ (acro.). These are shortened expressions formed from the initials of individual words.

AC, for example, can mean either "air conditioning" or "alternating current." AKA is short for "also known as." "ASAP" means "as soon as possible." An ATM is an automated teller machine at a bank. And these are just a few expressions that start with A!

There are thousands of others in common use, from EST (Eastern Standard Time, or the time zone on the eastern coast of the U.S.) and PIN (personal identification number) to VIP (very important person) and WTB (want to buy). One of the oddest is TEOTWAWKI (the end of the world as we know it)!

❶ An acronym is a set of initials formed by taking the first letter of each word in a group noun or set phrase (NIMBY = not in my back yard, NASA = National Aeronautics and Space Administration). What makes acronyms different from other initials is that they are pronounced as a word, not as separate letters. For example, NASA is pronounced [nǽsə] and NIMBY is pronounced [nímbi].

Sometimes a famous person's name gets shortened. President Franklin D. Roosevelt, for example, was "FDR." Many familiar, shortened names for government agencies in the U.S. began with his administration, such as "CCC" for Civilian Conservation Corps and "FDIC" for Federal Deposit Insurance Corporation. This practice has continued. HEW is the Department of Health, Education, and Welfare; FBI stands for the Federal Bureau of Investigation; and the Federal Communications Commission is the FCC.

Other presidents' names have been shortened also. President John F. Kennedy was widely known as "JFK." His successor, President Lyndon B. Johnson, was "LBJ."

Though such expressions can be confusing, they save a lot of time and effort. They also save space in print and on signs. DOT, for example, is quicker and easier to write than "Department of Transportation," and ETA is much shorter than "estimated time of arrival."

Abbreviations are used especially often in email, where people try to say a lot in a very short space. In 2004, for example, a survey showed that the most frequently used abbreviations online included NP (no problem), CB (call back), and TTYL (talk to you later). Then there is RFL. It means "ready for lunch"!

Whatever you can think of, Americans probably have an acronym or abbreviation related to it. In fact, their country itself is known as the USA!

 **WORDS FOR COMMUNICATIONS**

✓ acronym
✓ element
✓ initial
✓ survey
✓ usage
✓ widely

Questions

01   What is the overall tone of this passage? Is it light, serious, or critical? Give two reasons for your opinion.

02   Look at the word **curious** in the passage. What do you think **curious** means in this context?

03   What is the advantage of using acronyms and abbreviations?

The 21st Century: "Ebonics"

Does "ebonics" deserve to be called a language?

Around the year 2000, a controversy in American schools brought to mind an important question: what is "standard" American English? In this instance, the answer was not certain – and the uncertainty showed much about language as a reflection of America's social structure.

The controversy involved the speech of urban African-Americans. Some people thought that speech has a language itself, with its own special rules and vocabulary. It became known as "ebonics." That name was derived from the noun "ebony," meaning black, and the suffix "-onics," meaning a variety of speech.

In the late 20th century, many urban African-Americans had their own dialects, or variations on standard English. They had a special vocabulary, for example. "Ask," for example, became "axe." To "dis" something meant to criticize or mock it. "Neighborhood" became simply "hood," and "jet" meant to depart.

Many Americans thought such talk was much inferior to the "standard" English that most Americans spoke. People made fun of "ebonics" and treated it as crude, lower-class speech.

As the 21st century began, however, some Americans viewed this branch of American speech, with its seemingly strange vocabulary and grammar, in a different way. They saw it as a language in its own right, with its own special characteristics. It needed a name. The name they chose was "ebonics."

Defenders of "ebonics" thought it deserved the same status as ordinary English in America. In other words, it was not to be mocked, scorned, and rejected, but treated with respect.

Not everyone thought "ebonics" deserved such respect. A controversy arose. If "ebonics" came to be seen as **legitimate**, its critics wondered, then what was next? Could any dialect soon claim the status of a legitimate language?

In addition to the controversy concerning the future of the English language, there were also social considerations at work in the controversy over ebonics. Language is a powerful force in determining wealth and social status. If a person walked into an interview speaking a dialect that was seen as "low class" or inferior, that person's chances of getting a job would be hurt. So, stakes in the ebonics debate were high indeed.

❶ Here, *read* means "that is" or "in other words."

In the end, the ebonics movement did not get very far. Standard (read❶ white) English is still the language of power in America, and ebonics is still generally viewed as a lesser form of English. Still, it made an important point. Is "legitimate" versus "degenerate" language merely a matter of one's viewpoint, reflecting factors such as race and social class?

◁) ebonics [iːbɑniks]

📄 **WORDS FOR COMMUNICATIONS**
✓ claim
✓ controversy
✓ crude
✓ derive
✓ deserve
✓ dialect
✓ inferior
✓ legitimate
✓ reflection
✓ status

Questions

01   In your own words, explain the ebonics movement and its goals.

02   Look at the word **legitimate** in the passage. What do you think **legitimate** means in this context?

03   In this passage, what can you infer about race and social class in America?

5.10   The 21st Century: "Post-Literate" America

Are they growing up in a "post-literate" society?

America's literacy rate is dropping. This may seem strange. The U.S. is supposed to have one of the world's highest literacy rates. Yet, Americans, on the whole, do not read as much, or as well, as they used to.

It is now difficult for many Americans to read and understand the front page of a major newspaper such as the *New York Times*. Also, it is increasingly rare for Americans to read books. A study cited in *The Economist* in 2004 said that only 46.7 percent of Americans, or fewer than half, had read any "literature" (plays, fiction, or poetry) in 2002. That figure was **considerably** higher in 1992 (54 percent) and in 1982 (56.9 percent).

One can see this change reflected in books sold at newsstands. "When I was a teenager, 40 years ago," writes one widely published American writer, "you could go into an ordinary drugstore in an ordinary city and find works by Goethe and Shakespeare for sale, or a translation of a then current Russian novel. What do you find now?"

Content of magazines and newspapers is changing, too. Forty years ago, for example, a major U.S. magazine – not a literary magazine, but a news magazine sold everywhere – ran an article about the "mystery" of Mark Twain's novels.

Had someone else, the article asked, written his novels for him? Had Twain been only the "front," or mouthpiece❶, for some other writer who did not want his identity known? Was even the name "Mark Twain," which can be interpreted to mean, "See, there are two of us here," a subtle hint that a second author was involved in writing Twain's books?

One would have to look a long time to find articles like that now in

❶ A *front* or *mouthpiece* is a writer who is hired to present the ideas or work of another writer who does not want his or her name known. A famous person, for example, might hire a front or mouthpiece to present controversial ideas.

magazines for the average American. Articles then also were longer and had more advanced vocabulary than they do today. Many articles now are little more than captions for photos, and are written in the simplest language. People just do not wish (or are unable) to read anything more sophisticated.

Welcome to the "post-literate society." Some people think we are heading for, or already in, an age when literacy as we once knew it is no longer important. Is that view correct? Are Americans leaving literacy behind? Is "literacy" in the old sense already a thing of the past?

🔊 Goethe [gə́ːtə]

📑 **WORDS FOR COMMUNICATIONS**

✓ average
✓ considerably
✓ content
✓ identity
✓ interpret
✓ literacy
✓ major
✓ rare
✓ reflect
✓ sophisticated
✓ subtle

Questions

01   What point does the author make about American society? Explain in your own words.

02   Look at the word **considerably** in the passage. What do you think **considerably** means in this context?

03   Why do you think the author inserts the words "not a literary magazine, but a news magazine sold everywhere"? How do these words support the rest of the passage? Explain.

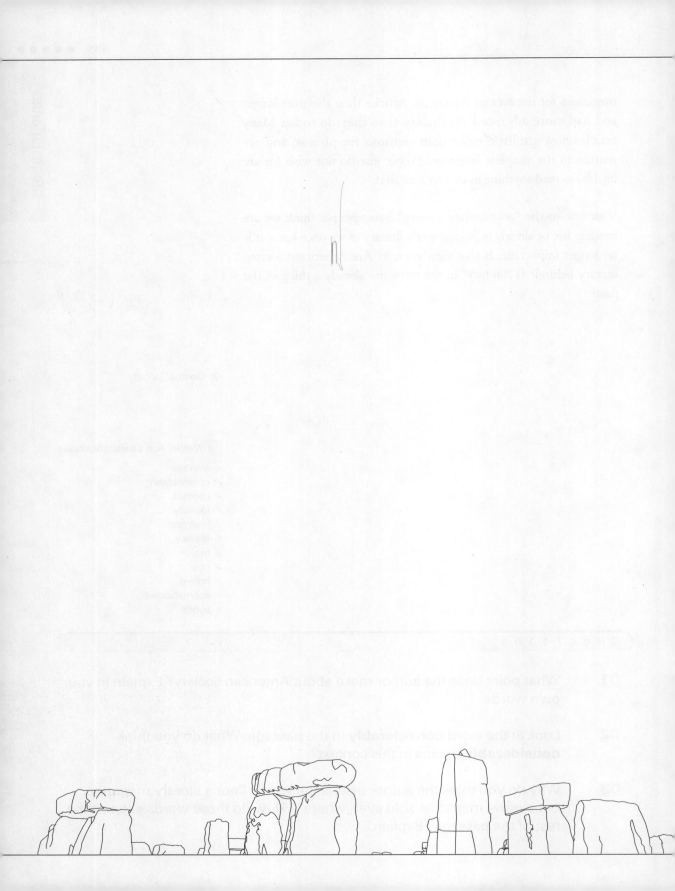

S O C I A L S C I E N C E S

Answer Key

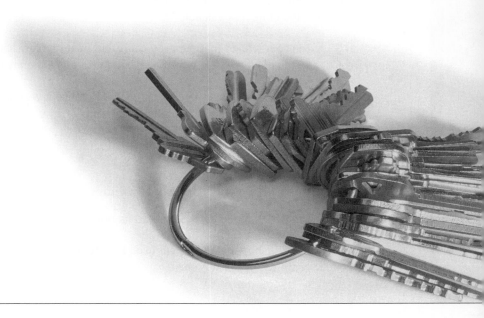

I. Basic **Economics**

 1.1 The 17th-18th Century: Wampum   p.09

01   A lining is the inside coating of an object. For example, your jacket has a lining on the inside.

02   Wampum was made from the insides of clam shells. Native Americans also used beads, minerals, and animal bones as money.

03   Wampum was used to conclude treaties and to show that a message from a tribe was official.

04   You can infer that the relationship between the Dutch colony and the Native Americans must have been relatively friendly because they had economic trade. You know this because the Dutch colony made use of wampum, which they must have gotten by trading with the Native Americans.

 1.2 The 18th Century: The Trouble with Paper Money   p.11

01   Skeptical means doubtful, or not trustful of something.

02   People refused to accept debased coins because they contained less gold or silver and were therefore less valuable.

03   The courts ruled that debased coins and paper money had the same value as gold coins, and thus enforced the government's right to make money in these forms.

04   Americans preferred the Spanish dollar because it was already in widespread use and it was made of gold or silver rather than simply paper.

 1.3 The 18th Century: Decimal Coinage   p.13

01   The British monetary system had its origins in ancient Rome.

02   The British monetary system used a system of fractions which made it difficult to perform math with English money.

03   Nickels, or half-dimes as they were called at the time, were the first coins issued in America.

04   You can infer that they were unsure of the half-dime's success since they only issued a small number of them.

05   The word derived means based on.

The 19th Century: Thorstein Veblen   p.15

01   Veblen's theory basically said that there was a conflict between people who were historically rich, such as powerful families and nobility, and people who became rich because they invented some new piece of technology. So basically, technology had the power to disrupt the social order as it had stood for hundreds of years.

02   The royal family of England, the Rockefellers of the United States, or the Saud family in Saudi Arabia would all be examples of the ceremonial element in Veblen's theory. All of these families are rich because they come from rich, powerful families and have been rich for many years. Bill Gates would be a good example of the technological element of Veblen's theory. Bill Gates was not wealthy until he created a new technology, the Microsoft operating system.

03   The word influential means to be socially or politically powerful.

The 19th Century: The "Free Silver" Movement   p.17

01   A measure is an action taken to solve a problem.

02   The object of the free silver movement was to lessen the value of the dollar so that farmers could pay off their debts more easily.

03   Farmers supported the free silver movement because they needed an easy way to pay off their debts. Silver miners supported the movement because changing to a silver currency would help their business. Banks opposed the free silver movement because if the farmers paid off their loans with silver, the banks would lose money.

04   The free-silver movement ended after its presidential candidate, William Jennings Bryan, lost the election. In addition, the economy improved shortly after that, so the free silver movement was no longer necessary.

1.6 The 19th-20th Century: Oil and the U.S. Economy   p.19

01   Whale oil was used for lighting homes and as a lubricant for machinery.

02   The whaling industry was such a central part of the US economy that it was the center of one of America's greatest novels.

03   The discovery of petroleum and cheap forms of fuel based on petroleum brought an end to the whaling industry.

04   The current energy problem is that the US is totally dependent on petroleum, and there are doubts about how much longer the world's supply of petroleum will last.

05   Exhaust means to use up or to use the last of something.

1.7 The 20th Century: What Started the Great Depression?   p.21

01   Americans felt that their economy would continue to grow and trusted the government to keep the stock market healthy.

02   People did not have much money, so they stopped buying things. Therefore, companies did not need as many workers to make products. Companies fired their extra workers, and people then had even less money to buy things. This process continued in a cycle.

03   Wiped out means completely destroyed.

1.8 The 20th Century: John Kenneth Galbraith   p.23

01   The word renowned means widely respected.

02   Galbraith believed that government needed to take a more active role in controlling the economy.

03   Galbraith's ideas helped to inspire the government's social spending programs in the 1960s.

04   Galbraith's critics said that his ideas were just a way to defend the government taking more power, and that he oversimplified the economy.

1.9 The 20th Century: Supply-Side Economics   p.25

01   Supply-side economics was supposed to help the lower and middle classes by bringing more money to the upper class, who would then spend more money on the services that the middle and lower classes provided.

02   The Reagan administration cut taxes and eased regulations on businesses to make it easier for them to operate.

03   Supply-side economics did improve the economy, but it also increased the differences between the rich and the poor, and the tax cuts also contributed to the national deficit.

04   Doldrums is a noun that describes a time or condition of slow growth or inactivity.

II. Political **Science**

2.1 The 18th Century: Thomas Jefferson and the Declaration of Independence   p.29

01   Jefferson was more interested in writing the constitution for the state of Virginia.

02   Jefferson used the Virginia Declaration of Rights and his own drafts for the Virginia Constitution as sources.

03   Jefferson showed his first draft to the other members of the constitutional committee, who then made suggestions. The second draft was then taken to the Continental Congress, where it was finalized.

04   Equivalent means something that is basically the same as another thing. Here, Jefferson's portable desk served basically the same purpose that a laptop would serve today.

2.2 The 18th Century: Separation of Powers   p.31

01   The writers of the U.S. Constitution were afraid that one person or group would gain too much power in government.

02   They got the basic idea from the ancient Greeks and the specific details from Montesquieu.

03   The legislative branch creates laws. The executive branch enforces the laws. The judicial branch interprets the laws.

04   A tyranny is government which has total, and unjust, power over its citizens.

2.3 The 18th-20th Century: The Two-Party System   p.33

01   According to the passage, Americans prefer the two-party system because it simplifies their choices during an election.

02   The ratification of the Constitution caused the formation of the two-party system because there were two groups with opposing views on how the Constitution should be written.

03 The Federalists wanted a strong federal government. The Anti-federalists wanted a weaker federal government, more power for the states, and a bill of rights in the Constitution.

04 Wary means to be careful or cautious of something.

05 It is difficult for third parties to gain power in the U.S. because the two main parties are extremely powerful, and third parties often join with one of the two main parties during elections.

 The 18th-20th Century: **Who Elects a President?** p.35

01 In a U.S. presidential election, the president is actually selected by representatives rather than by a popular vote.

02 In this context, framers means writers or makers.

03 The Americans got the idea for the Electoral College from the ancient Romans.

04 One problem caused by the Electoral College occurred in the 1800 election, when the electoral vote was tied and Congress had to choose the president.

 The 18th-21st Century: **Who Are "We the People"?** p.37

01 The word elusive means hard to catch or hard to find.

02 Americans assume that the words "We the people" have always included everyone in America. This is actually not the case. When the Constitution was first written, full rights of citizenship were only extended to white males who owned property.

 The 19th Century: **The Rise and Fall of Populism** p.39

01 The word discredit means to make someone look as if they should not be trusted or believed.

02 The populists wanted more power for average people in government.

03   Farmers supported the populist movement because they wanted easier ways to pay off their debts.

04   Two things hurt the populists. First their language was too radical, so they seemed like extremists. In addition, after they joined with the Democratic Party for the 1896 elections, they no longer seemed to have an individual voice.

2.7   The 19th Century: **Disputed Elections**   p.41

01   The word bloodshed means violence, usually violence that results in the loss of life.

02   The dispute in the 1876 election was caused by the difference in the results of the popular vote and the electoral vote. Tilden won the popular vote, but the results of the electoral vote were unclear because each side accused the other side of cheating in the election.

03   It was important to resolve the dispute because the government could not operate without a president. In addition, Tilden's supporters were threatening to use violence to make him the president, and no one wanted to have another civil war.

04   The Republicans and Democrats reached a secret deal in which Hayes became president in return for promising to remove all federal troops from the South.

2.8   The 19th-21st Century: **Positive versus Negative Politics**   p.43

01   The phrase born of means caused by or created by.

02   In negative politics, candidates criticize something without offering a solution. They simply oppose something, but they do not offer an alternative.

03   The Know-nothing movement was an example of negative politics because its entire objective was to oppose immigration by European Roman Catholics.

04   The largest weakness of negative politics is that it is the product of fears that usually do not last long.

2.9   The 20th Century: **Was Roosevelt's "New Deal" a Good Idea?**   p.45

01 The New Deal was a group of social programs that were designed to improve the economy and lessen the differences between the rich and the poor in America.

02 The New Deal failed largely because it tried to do too many things.

03 In this context, mobilized describes the action of preparing for something; in this case, preparing for a war by making weapons.

04 The New Deal created the Social Security system and made people more accepting of a large federal government.

2.10 The 20th Century: When Are "Rights" Wrong? p.47

01 This quote illustrates the conflict of rights by showing how one person's rights may cause harm to another person.

02 The word endanger means to put someone or something at risk of harm.

2.11 The 20th Century: The Lobbying Industry p.49

01 A lobby is a group whose goal is to influence the government in some way. For example, a lobby may want the government to pass a law regarding a certain issue.

02 Lobbies give the rich an advantage because lobbying is very expensive. Since the rich can afford to do more lobbying, they have a greater voice in the government.

03 The word consideration means concern, or something to be thought about.

III. Psychology

3.1 Ancient Times-the 21st Century: What Folk Heroes Tell Us   p.53

01   The main point of this passage is that you can learn a lot about a culture by examining its folk heroes.

02   Paul Bunyan reflects American thinking because everything about Paul Bunyan is big, which is how Americans often see their country. In addition, Paul Bunyan displays many of the qualities that Americans see in themselves.

03   The word counterpart means something that plays the same role or has the same function. For example, the prime minister in England and the president in America are counterparts. These two people serve the same function in government.

3.2 The 18th-21st Century: National Villains   p.55

01   According to the passage, every society needs villains to serve as a contrast to its heroes.

02   The word unique means that something is the only one of its kind; that there are no other things like it.

03   The paragraph seems to suggest that the American hatred of Arnold has more to do with the need to have villains than with Arnold's actual treachery.

3.3 The 19th Century: The Lincoln Cult   p.57

01   According to the passage, Lincoln was not nearly as respected during his lifetime as his legend would seem to suggest.

02   In this context, obscure means unknown or not famous.

03   The author suggests that Lincoln's popularity was caused by the need for a figure that would unite the country again after the civil war.

3.4 The 19th-21st Century: The Elusive "American Character"   p.59

01   The author makes the point that the only truly unified aspect of the American character is a submission to technology.

02   The author claims that over the last 100 years, Americans have let machines do more and more of their thinking for them.

03   The author seems to take a negative view of the changes in American society. The author describes Americans as being "programmed." This is a very negative portrayal.

04   The word subservience means submission.

3.5 The 19th-20th Century: Americans and "Aliens"   p.61

01   The author makes the point that anti-immigrant feelings in America are generally short-lived, and after a time, the new immigrants are accepted.

02   The author uses these names because they represent people from different cultures. The author uses them to make the point that eventually new immigrants mixed together and were accepted in America.

3.6 The 19th-20th Century: The Importance of Uncle Sam   p.63

01   Uncle Sam is an easily recognizable image. In addition, there is no copyright on his image, so many people use it.

02   The author mentions these characters because they are known around the world. By comparing Uncle Sam to them, the author is pointing out that Uncle Sam is an extremely well-known character as well.

03   Copyright is the legal protection given to the creator of an image or piece of writing to ensure that other people do not use it without the creator's permission.

04   The author suggests that Uncle Sam had his origins in a meat inspector named Samuel Wilson, who looked a great deal like the character. The barrels of meat he inspected were marked "U.S.," and people joked that it stood for Uncle Sam, a play on his name.

3.7 The 19th-20th Century: The Need for a Frontier   p.65

01   According to the passage, a frontier has become a necéssary part of American thinking. When Americans have not had a frontier, they have tended to invent one or think back to a time when there was a frontier.

02   A mainstay is an essential part of something.

03   According to the passage, after they completed the western expansion, Americans were troubled that they no longer had a frontier. In response, they became nostalgic for the old west and created a romanticized view of it.

3.8 The 20th Century: "Star Trek" and American Thinking   p.67

01   The author points out that the TV show emerged at the same time as President Kennedy spoke about a "new frontier."

02   The show reflects the American need for a frontier of some kind. It also reflects the multiculturalism of America, the mixed feelings of Americans for technology, and the qualities that Americans respect in a leader.

03   Captain Kirk is a popular character in America because people enjoy watching him make difficult decisions. They like this because they like to imagine what they would do in that situation.

04   The word authoritarian describes a government that has great control over the private lives of its citizens.

3.9 The 20th Century: Shaping Public Opinion   p.69

01   A public opinion survey is a study which asks a number of people for their opinion about a certain subject. The objective is to predict what society as a whole thinks about that subject based on the answers of those people.

02   A poll is a kind of survey.

03   People seek to manipulate opinion polls because opinion polls can influence public opinion. People can manipulate opinion polls by using selected quotes that distort other people's true opinions or by asking questions that are misleading.

04   The author mentions a ship to show that even though a single opinion poll may have a small effect on public opinion, over time, many opinion polls can have a large combined effect. In this sense, the ship represents public opinion.

3.10 The 20th Century: How To Sell Anything   p.71

01   Advertising is important in America because selling things is an essential part of the American economy.

02   Advertisers use words, images, and sounds in their advertisements.

03   You can infer that an effective slogan should be short. It should also rhyme so that it is easy to remember.

04   The word crafted means made, but it is usually used when something is made with special care and effort.

3.11 The 20th Century: The UFO Phenomenon   p.73

01   After World War II, many people just wanted peace. The fear that there could soon be a war with an alien race contributed to the interest in UFOs.

02   The word foes means enemies.

03   Hollywood made two kinds of movies about aliens. Movies such as *Earth versus the Flying Saucers* portrayed aliens that were hostile. Movies such as *E.T.* portrayed friendly aliens.

3.12 The 20th Century: "Environmental Awareness"   p.75

01   The large size of America led Americans to believe that they could exploit the environment because it seemed like there would always be plenty of natural resources. Their viewpoint started to change in the second half of the 20th century when they saw that this was not the case.

02   The author believes that environmental awareness has been misused in America and is now more of a marketing tool than an attempt to preserve the environment.

03   The word prevailed means was dominant.

3.13 The 20th Century: **Americans and the "Underdog"**   p.77

01   The author mentions baseball because it is a typical example of a situation in which Americans often prefer the underdog.

02   The word underlies means to form the basis of something.

03   America's fascination with the underdog is rooted in its experience in the Revolutionary War, in which it was the underdog.

IV. Sociology

4.1 The 18th-20th Century: "Equality" and Reality   p.81

01   The main point of the passage is that while Americans like to view themselves as a society based on equality, their society has been very unequal for much of its history.

02   The word distinction means difference.

03   The author makes the point that while slavery was made illegal, the work conditions for many laborers were not much better than they had been for the slaves.

4.2 The 19th Century: The Politics of Corruption   p.83

01   Tweed was able to gain a great deal of power because he had powerful friends and because he helped immigrants, who voted for him in return.

02   This quote shows that Tweed felt that he was above the law and could not be punished.

03   The word looted means stole from.

04   One of his men felt he was not getting enough of the stolen money and betrayed Tweed.

4.3 The 19th-20th Century: The Irish in America   p.85

01   The word inseparable describes two things that are so closely connected that they can never be separated.

02   Poverty in Ireland and the potato famine brought large numbers of Irish immigrants to America.

03   The author mentions these names to illustrate how common the descendants of Irish immigrants are in America.

4.4 The 19th-20th Century: **The Japanese-American Experience** p.87

01 Japanese immigration started in 1868 with a group of Japanese farmers who came to work on sugar plantations in Hawaii.

02 It was after the surprise attack on Pearl Harbor that Japanese Americans were placed in internment camps.

03 The word internee refers to a person who was placed in an internment camp.

04 The major difference is that European immigrants were accepted much more quickly than Japanese immigrants. The European immigrants were not under the same immigration controls as Japanese immigrants, and they were never placed in interment camps, despite the fact that some of them came from countries that the US was at war with.

 4.5 The 20th Century: **America's Urban Underclass** p.89

01 The growth of the underclass has been caused by the growth of technology, which has replaced many of the jobs that uneducated people did before. In addition, many mentally ill people were released from hospitals in the 1980s, and many of these people are too sick to hold jobs.

02 Wind up means to finally arrive at a situation.

03 According to the author, talking to the homeless teaches one that many of the homeless were once middle class people before some misfortune caused them to lose their jobs and their homes.

 4.6 The 20th Century: **Class Lines** p.91

01 The expression cash-poor describes a state in which a person does not have money readily available. For example, a person could own a large home and not be poor because he or she could sell the home. But that person might be cash-poor because it would take time to sell the home.

02 Class is sometimes hard to define because there are many different minor distinctions within classes. In addition, wealth can be calculated in many ways, making it difficult to define one's social class.

03 According to the passage, an understanding of their social status is important to Americans because it helps them understand their place in society.

The 20ᵗʰ Century: How Real Is the "American Dream"?   p.93

01 The comparison suggests that like the nightclub, the American dream may no longer exist.

02 The author mentions Horatio Alger because much of his writing was about people fulfilling the American dream.

03 In this context, the word foundation means basis.

04 The author has a positive view of the American dream. You know this because he spends a lot of time defending the American dream and proving that it is more than just an illusion.

The 20ᵗʰ Century: The Academic Class   p.95

01 The word dedicate means to devote oneself to something.

02 The images of a wall and a tower reinforce the separation that used to exist between the academic class and average people.

03 Radio and television contributed to the rising popularity of academics because television and radio programs always needed new and interesting stories.

The 20ᵗʰ Century: Superstar Scientists   p.97

01 In order to become superstars, scientists need to be relatively attractive and they need to be able to explain their research in simple terms.

02 The author implies that most scientists do not make a lot of money.

03 In this context, stellar means great or very famous.

04 Some people object to scientists becoming superstars because they feel that it takes attention away from other scientists who are doing important work but are not

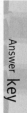

Answer key

good at speaking to the media.

 The 20th Century: **The Effects of Automation**   p.99

01   The two major negative effects of automation on American society have been the loss of jobs to machines and the loss of control in some aspects of Americans' lives.

02   The word grand means large or huge.

03   Many science fiction stories and movies dealt with situations in which society's dependence on technology became a problem. One example mentioned in the passage is a short story in which a city is thrown into chaos when all the traffic lights turn green at the same time.

 The 20th Century: **Conformists and Rebels**   p.101

01   In pop culture, rebels are usually young, searching for a new way of life, and often meet with a sad end.

02   The word heyday describes the height of someone's fame. It is the time at which someone is most popular.

03   According to the passage, rebels and conformists need each other. Rebels need conformists because without them, there would be nothing to rebel against. Conformists need rebels because the bad things that happened to the rebels confirm the conformists' belief in sticking to the norm.

 The 20th Century: **The 1960s Counterculture**   p.103

01   The counterculture was the culture that young people in the 1960s created to rebel against their parents. It mainly emphasized individuality.

02   The older generation viewed the counterculture as a simple rebellion against society's values. The younger generation saw the counterculture largely as a pursuit of freedom.

03   The word norm describes the behaviors and beliefs that are considered normal and acceptable by society.

04   The author is pointing out that in some ways, the counterculture went against its own beliefs because it created its own norms that its members were expected to conform to.

 The 20th Century: Schools — What Do You Get for Your Money?   p.105

01   Americans pay high tuition fees to go to top schools because attending those schools puts them in contact with a network of rich and powerful people.

02   The word sums means amounts of money.

 The 20th-21st Century: Who Should Pay for Public Schools?   p.107

01   This passage is about the differences between schools in rich and poor areas in America, the problems these differences cause, and possible solutions to these problems.

02   The expression worlds apart is used to describe two things that are so different that they might as well be on different planets.

03   The differences in public schools are caused by the fact that public schools are funded by local taxes. Rich areas get more tax money, so they can build better schools.

04   One possible solution suggested by the author is to take school funding from a statewide tax that would be distributed evenly among all schools.

 The 20th-21st Century: A Society on Drugs   p.109

01   The author mentions Al Capone because he got rich selling alcohol illegally. This shows how historically ineffective American attempts to stop its drug culture have been.

02   A loophole is an ineffective part of a law. Sometimes people can avoid having to follow a law because it was written poorly. This is a loophole.

03   The U.S. has found it difficult to stop drug usage because loopholes in the law have allowed people to change a drug slightly and continue to sell it. In addition, prescription drugs are widely available in the U.S. Finally, the widespread acceptance of "recreational drug use" in America has made it difficult to stop drug usage.

4.16 The 21st Century: Los Angeles Ignites   p.111

01   The L.A. riots showed Americans that their society had not made as much progress towards equality as they thought it had.

02   The author seems to suggest that television coverage of the King trial contributed to the L.A. riots. You know this because the author makes a point of noting that the verdict was shown on national television just before the riots started.

03   The phrase hard to swallow means difficult to believe.

04   According to the author, the main cause of the L.A. riots was racial inequality. The author suggests that the King verdict was simply the event that exposed preexisting anger.

4.17 The 21st Century: Is the "Melting Pot" an Illusion?   p.113

01   The concept of America as a melting pot is the idea that after immigrants come to America, they take on the characteristics of American culture until they are indistinguishable from other Americans.

02   The major problem with the melting pot model is that some immigrants do not wish to fully integrate into American culture. They want to keep their original culture as a separate and distinct culture.

03   The word assimilate means to become a part of another culture and to fully mix into that new culture.

04   Some immigrants dislike some parts of American culture and do not want to assimilate into a culture they see as immoral.

V.   Communications

5.1   The 19th-21st Century: "Ameringlish" vs. "Britglish"   p.117

01   American and British English often differ in spellings, such as color and colour. They also sometimes differ in verb conjugations. Americans say "have gotten," but the British say "have got."

02   Diverged means to have moved away or to have separated.

03   The author's purpose in this passage is to discuss some of the ways in which American English and British English have diverged in the 200 years since America became an independent country.

5.2   The 20th-21st Century: The Decline of the Letter   p.119

01   One reason for the decline of the letter was the invention of the telephone. Telephones provided an easier and faster way to communicate than letters. Later, email made letters even more unnecessary.

02   Letters are important to historians because they tell them a lot about what life was like at a certain time.

03   The expression free fall describes a situation in which something is declining very rapidly.

5.3   The 20th Century: The Video Age Begins   p.121

01   One major reason is that people spent far more time watching television than they did watching movies.

02   The word immersed means to be surrounded by something.

03   It tells you that choosing the right images to communicate an idea became very important in the television era.

5.4 The 20th Century: Spanglish   p.123

01   Calquing means when a word from one language gets used in a different language, but in a slightly different form.

02   The word oral in this context means spoken.

03   The author mentions Chinglish and Konglish. One would expect to hear these languages in parts of America with large numbers of Chinese or Korean immigrants as well as in China and Korea.

5.5 The 20th Century: Communication by Song   p.125

01   The author mentions Zelda Fitzgerald in order to show that music lyrics have been important in America for a long time.

02   The expression fed up describes a feeling in which people have become so frustrated or angry that they can no longer stand it.

03   The controversy centered around a song in which Ice-T sang about violence against police officers as a form of revenge. Some people thought Ice-T was wrong to make the song because they believed it would encourage people to use violence against the police. Other people thought the song was an expression of free speech and showed the anger that many young people felt towards police officers.

5.6 The 20th Century: The Internet and Language   p.127

01   The term originated from the word hacker, which meant a person who was proficient in computer use.

02   The word conventions means the established rules of usage.

03   The main advantage of haxor-speak is that it is faster than typing full words. The main disadvantage is that not everyone understands it.

04   The last sentence is simply a humorous way of ending the passage.

5.7 The 20th Century: American Slang   p.129

01 One example is aerospew, which means to talk a lot without saying anything important. Another example is zilch, which means zero, or nothing.

02 One way slang is created is when an ordinary word is taken and used in a new way. Another way to create slang is to combine different parts of words to make a new word.

03 In this context, substance means importance.

5.8 The 20th-21st Century: Acro., Abbr., & Everyday Speech   p.131

01 The tone of this passage is light (not serious). You can tell this by the last sentence of the passage, which ends in a little joke. In addition, the author uses exclamation points in several places where they are not really necessary. This is usually an indication of a light tone.

02 In this context, curious means strange or odd.

03 The major advantage of using acronyms and abbreviations is that they save time and space.

5.9 The 21st Century: "Ebonics"   p.133

01 The ebonics movement was a movement to get the African-American dialect to be seen as more acceptable in society. This was important because the view that ebonics was an uneducated, inferior dialect placed African-Americans at a disadvantage in society.

02 Legitimate means accepted or recognized.

03 Based on the information in the passage, you can infer that race is strongly related to social class in America. You know this because if African-Americans were generally of the same social class as white Americans, the ebonics movement would not have been necessary.

5.10 The 21st Century: "Post-Literate" America   p.135

01 The author points out that Americans are becoming less literate and reading less.

02 The word considerably means significantly.

03 This shows how much more literate American society used to be.

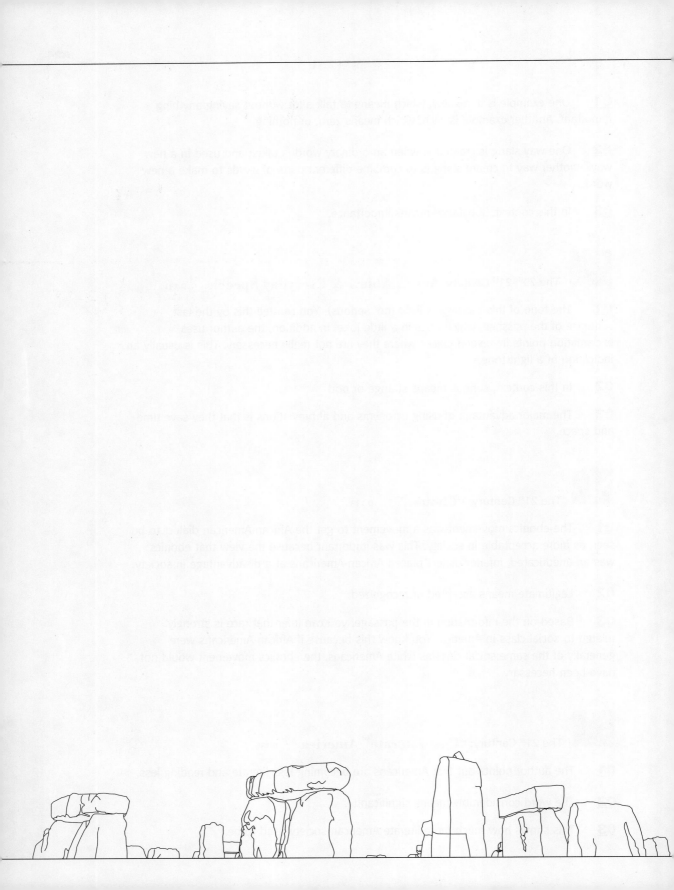

SOCIAL SCIENCES
Index

Index

NOTE: Index entries are derived from the topic word lists in each passage.

Index

NOTE: Index entries are derived from the topic word lists in each passage.